A LIFE IN MEDICINE

A Biography of

Malachy Smyth, M.D., F.A.C.S., F.R.C.S.

by

Aubrey Malone

Web Publications, 2005

© Aubrey Malone

ISBN: 0 952 8009 2 6

Printed and bound by Colour Books Ltd., Baldoyle

Acknowledgements

Shortly after this book went to press, the tsunami wave catastrophe took place in Asia. Dr Smyth, as a result, has kindly agreed to pledge all profits from sales to the Irish Red Cross at 16 Merrion Square, Dublin 2 to put towards fundraising.

He would like to dedicate the book to his deceased wife Lucy, and to all the O'Hara clan.

It has been written in cooperation with *Senior Times*, Ireland's premier magazine for the elderly. The author would like to thank Des Duggan, the publisher of *Senior Times*, for his help and advice, and Conor O'Hagan for his artwork.

The author would also like to thank Jeffrey Taplin for his endless patience in processing the manuscript over its many sea-changes. As ever, he worked tirelessly against the clock without any complaints.

Introduction

To abolish pain dramatically is one of the most satisfying achievements of a clinician's life. The goal is seldom realized without a thorough understanding of the cause of pain. It was one of the outstanding achievements of Dr Smyth's varied career that he did just that. At a time when doctors were recognizing that much back pain, often described as 'lumbago' or 'sciatica' (descriptions, not diagnosis), could be due to a derangement of the lumbar intervertebral disc, he provided the definitive experiment that showed this was so. A combination of Irish imagination, rigorous surgical technique and the enthusiasm of youth, found ways of demonstrating, beyond doubt, the cause of pain in these patients – and even more important, how the pain could be eradicated. The importance of his definitive paper on the subject was recognized by its being reprinted and published as a classic in *Clinical Orthopedics and Related Research* (volume 29 1977). This fundamental work is the basis on which modern techniques of lumbar disc surgery have developed. It has made back surgery a very limited procedure and allowed patients to go home in a few days after disc operation. First class sportsmen, earning millions of dollars, have been able to go back to top class athletics or football.

The details of these experiments are vividly described in this volume. They are delightfully set against the background of a colourful life, which gives warm insights into Irish, British and American culture.

Verna Wright
Professor of Rheumatology
University of Leeds

1

The term 'Monaghan' comes from the Irish 'muineachán', which means 'a hilly place'. There are many such hills around the area which have been immortalised by the county's most acclaimed poet, Patrick Kavanagh. It was chosen as the site of the county's principal town as far back as the 16th century.

Its population at the end of the 19th century was 2,932, which was 30% lower than it had been before the Famine. But it was still a prosperous market town, drawing farmers to its fairs from the surrounding counties of Tyrone and Armagh. Its shops provided employment at a time when jobs were scarce and emigration rampant. An apprenticeship in a Monaghan store was a goal to be aspired to. The town was also an important administrative centre with a growing number of professional people. Every year saw at least one new house built there.

In 1911 about a quarter of the Monaghan people were Protestants. These were divided equally between Church of Ireland and Presbyterian, with a few hundred Methodists. They owned land out of all proportion to their numbers and also occupied positions of importance within the county. Many of them were Orangemen and UVF members. They were vehemently opposed to Home Rule for obvious reasons. They feared they would be the butt of much acrimony, if not violence, in a Catholic-dominated Ireland.

They were also obviously worried about the growing power of Sinn Féin, despite the fact that the Sinn Féin TD Ernest Blythe, who would be elected in 1918, was himself a Protestant. In some parts of Monaghan, the north particularly, they acted as a fifth column in their efforts to thwart the IRA, giving assistance to Crown forces wherever possible. In 1916, however, Ulster Unionists effectively 'disowned' Monaghan Protestants, abandoning them to the tender mercies of the newly-formed Irish government. Two years later, in a fit of pique at this train of events, Monaghan delegates withdrew from the Ulster Unionist Council.

In September 1919 the British government issued an order suppressing Dáil Éireann. The Volunteers, in retaliation, launched a campaign to destroy the last remnants of British administration in Ireland. There were frequent attacks on Crown forces throughout the country, forcing them to withdraw to the garrison towns, and only emerge in daylight for fear of sniper fire. 'Ireland was ours after dark,' said Paddy Corrigan, the captain of the Lisdoon company. But many IRA attacks on the Crown forces in these garrison towns proved futile, especially if there was a significant Black and Tan presence.

All of this made the Unionist population more determined than ever to resist inclusion under the Irish government. There was a virtual pogrom against Catholics right throughout the North. As a reaction to this, many people in Monaghan started to boycott Belfast goods coming into their town. In September 1920 Dáil Éireann officially ratified this policy and the boycott was strictly enforced by the Volunteers. Many Unionist traders refused to comply with it, which meant the campaign was stepped up. Goods entering Monaghan both by road and rail were blocked. Many trains were emptied of their goods, which were then destroyed. Sometimes trains were burned out. Checkpoints were also set up on the roads, though this was dangerous as carts were sometimes accompanied by armed auxiliaries. These had orders to shoot any roadblockers on sight.

Towards the end of the year British rule there was practically non-existent. The Sinn Féin courts took over from the British ones and the Sinn Féin police replaced the RIC in fighting crime. The local councils also supported the Republic, with the county's MPs boycotting Westminster in favour of the Dáil. The RIC had disintegrated by now, many of their members resigning while others shifted their loyalties to supply the Volunteers with valuable information.

At this time the Protestants were still entrenched in their own enclaves. They sang 'God Save the King' in their churches and sold poppies. They voted unanimously for their own Dáil candidates. For the first ten years of partition they brought the aforementioned Ernest Blythe to ministerial status despite the fact that they knew precious little about him. They also retained their membership of the Orange Order and the Royal Black Institution, holding annual demonstrations as if the Old Firm still held sway. They no longer marched under the Union Jack but it hadn't yet been replaced by the tricolour. In fact the Twelfth of July demonstration in Monaghan in 1924 was the biggest since 1910, over forty bands participating.

The following year, however, many Protestants complained that they weren't getting their fair share of public appointments. The Blueshirts had become prominent by now and had started to make their disapproval of Orange gatherings in the town manifest. Things came to a head on the Twelfth of July, the IRA stating that any parades would be deemed to be imperialistic and divisive. In some Monaghan towns that year, Republicans armed with hurleys and pitchforks broke into Orange halls and wrecked them. Baton charges from gardaí followed, and stand-offs developed. Similar stand-offs were prevalent in towns like Cootehill and Castleblaney. Some Monaghan members of Orange and Black orders found they had to travel to the north to march without fear of reprisals.

Negotiations, meanwhile, went on regarding the country in general. Across the water, David Lloyd George said that dealing with De Valera was like trying to pick up mercury with a fork. De Valera riposted, 'Then why doesn't he use a knife?' As far as Lloyd George was concerned, everytime Britain found an answer to 'the Irish Question', the Irish changed the question.

As the years went on, the local councillors in Monaghan tended to give the attractive jobs and houses to Catholics rather than Protestants. The Sisters of Mercy also came to Monaghan County Hospital. Protestant councillors complained but their grievances fell on deaf ears.

Ireland was changing, the downtrodden people of yesteryear crawling out from under the stone of the past. Factories also started to be set up, and roads repaired. The county was being born again.

Other developments followed in quick succession. Electricity came in, at first being seen almost as a miraculous innovation and then being taken for granted in time, like all innovations. Public buildings started to mushroom. A county hospital was built in Monaghan and a county home in Castleblaney. Cars became more common on the roads, and the county got its first bus service.

By 1932 the Catholics of Monaghan decorated their homes for the Eucharistic Congress and the streets were also decorated, as if to further emphasise that the town was now becoming a Catholic stronghold.

Malachy Smyth was born outside the town during World War I. He watched all these changes taking place as he grew up. What most influenced him was the number of soldiers leaving the town. They seemed to do so in an almost ghost-like manner. One minute they were there and then they weren't, like a vanishing act. The civilian Protestants were going too, but perhaps not as dramatically.

From the early years of the Free State there had been a certain amount of Protestant migration to the North and Britain but many were reluctant to leave their homes, feeling a move to Britain or the six counties would hurt them both financially and emotionally. Their young people still held an advantage over Catholics when it came to getting jobs. There were many large Protestant shops in the town as well as banks, and the Great Northern Railway. Many also felt the border was just a temporary thing.

The proximity of Northern Ireland was responsible for many of the departures. Protestants felt they might be more at home there in the new political climate, among their relatives and friends. The Unionists also encouraged them to leave. They wanted them to occupy farms and businesses that might otherwise fall to Catholics. The more people went, the more that wanted to go. They felt their ranks were depleted. It was like the domino principle. Some even went because they believed they had a better chance of meeting a marriage partner of their own religion further north. Mixed marriages caused a whole new raft of problems, with many more evacuations following as a result.

As Malachy grew up he noticed the absence of former residents in a number of ways. He peered through the windows of houses and saw nothing but the four walls, as if their inhabitants had been plucked away by some invisible force. There was an ominous silence in the air, as if something terrible had just taken place that he wasn't a party to. Why had these people gone? And where to?

Household pets were even absent. No dogs roamed about, or rent the air with their howling. No cattle grazed. The fields, like the country itself, seemed suddenly bereft of activity. A train passed occasionally, like something on the edges of memory.

It was the absence of the soldiers, though, that made the deepest impact on him. He saw discarded uniforms here and there, the last remaining vestiges of a vanquished army. They were being uprooted from the very soil from which their own ancestors uprooted the Irish themselves 700 years before. The hunters had suddenly become the hunted, the wheel of history turned full circle.

In the shops his enquiries as to the whereabouts of the soldiers were met by blank stares. 'I don't know where they've gone; they left no forwarding address.' Was there something he wasn't being told? Maybe people were still nervous, the after-shock of terror. But to him they were already the Forgotten People.

Like a giant thaw after a long winter, water seeped through the pipes again and the icy grip relaxed. He watched weeds stuffing themselves up through concrete pathways, watched thin men with frightened faces peer through curtains onto the empty, rain-drenched streets. Soon it would be safe to come out, to breathe the free air again. No more searches, no more bayonets, no more dark looks from strangers merely because you happened to pass them by on the street.

One day, for no reason in particular, he decided to go to the house of Pastor Carhalton, where he used to play as a child. It was a sombre building with leaded windows. A moss-covered avenue led up to it. There was no grass on the driveway, a path ridged through it from his daily excursions up and down, dressed in his dome-shaped black hat with the wide brim. His routines were almost as predictable as his philosophy of life. Could he be gone too?

The door was open when he got there and he entered from habit. There was always noise here, a meal being announced, visitors coming and going, the pastor's own stentorian voice. Today, though, nothing but the cawing of crows from the beech tree outside.

Then all of a sudden a jackdaw swooped down over his head and out the door. It was like a premonition. He opened the library door and walked in, and it was then he saw him, slouched in a chair at the window with his chin on his chest. His right hand was resting on an open book, his left one bent across his chest. A long strand of ivy crawled through the open window like a claw.

Malachy called out to him but there was no answer. When he moved closer to him he saw that his face was ashen blue. There was no breath coming out of his mouth. He was dead.

After the initial shock subsided he found himself staring at him instead of running away. He became an item of curiosity to him rather than a corpse. All memories drained from him of the man in human form. He wondered what his last thoughts had been, how much he'd suffered, if he'd had time to reach out to somebody for help. It was almost like a storybook death, like something from a novel. He looked strangely peaceful, as if he didn't put up any struggle at all. Could anybody, even a pastor, pass into eternity with such apparent nonchalance? Maybe such nonchalance typified Protestants.

His death was like a metaphor for the departure of all of his stock. Here was a man who refused to leave but he was taken too. The last man standing – or sitting. His life ebbed out of him like candle from a flame.

His body was eventually taken to the local hospital. It turned out he had lung cancer. Malachy thought of the cancer and the ivy eating away at different parts of him, claiming him for themselves. It was his first experience of death and he felt impotent about it. A pastor had died, that was all you could say. There were no last minute cures, no blaring ambulances, no life-saving surgery performed by a man who would have known just what action to take.

Malachy's future direction in life would be much influenced by this single image of an old man in wire-rimmed spectacles sprawled across a chair on a dark autumn afternoon, cancer invading him from inside and a long tentacle of ivy from outside.

2

Malachy's father was a teacher by trade but he also worked as a land surveyor. As the British left, economic opportunity increased. Houses were being sold faster than one could buy them by settlers pawning off what they'd never really owned in the first place. His father snapped up six of these houses which had previously been owned by the local English landlord.

Mickey Kirk was his name. Malachy remembers him as a wizened man riding an ancient bicycle almost as big as himself. He wore a dark suit that was green with age and a cap with its peak pointing rigidly ahead. Black hobnailed boots completed his fearsome gait.

He had acquired an air of bossiness and authority from his English masters in 'The Big House.' The tenants had to have the exact rent ready every week when he appeared on their doorsteps. The rent was two shillings and sixpence, payable on the nail. At that time there were two hundred and forty pennies in a pound and a pound was worth much more than today. The silver coins collected by Mickey Kirk kept the English lord languishing in his London club,

Malachy's father was known as The Master, but not in the same way the English landlords had been. He was a respected figure of some status over much of the area, a wise man to whom everyone came to consult about one thing or another, usually to get his help and advice for nothing. He was one of the biggest multispeciality consultants who was paid the smallest honorarium in the whole county. There was a continual stream of people pouring in to see him, as if he was Monaghan's answer to Don Corleone. But nobody woke up with a horse's head in their bed in this neck of the woods.

He had no office as such. Transactions took place in his house, counterpointed by the loud knock on the door, the barking of the dog, the conspiratorial *tête-à-tête* and then the shaking of hands before the visitors shuffled down the driveway. Afterwards the dog would look around almost apologetically as if to say, 'I'm sorry I made such a fuss, but what else is a dog to do?'

The local baker acted as his intermediary during auctions. He had strict instructions never to go above £100, no matter what the property. All of this resulted in the family moving to a bigger house half a mile from the village. It stood on a mound at the end of a long driveway, two great iron gates guarding the entrance and ancient oaks reaching out their long limbs like bodyguards.

In a sense it was as if the land had finally been returned to its rightful heirs. The Old Enemy had departed, but not without leaving some evidence of his presence because on one of the windows there were three bullet holes. Malachy was informed that these were 'gentle hints' to the previous owners to hasten their departure.

All of the family went to the local schools first but then dispersed. One of his brothers joined a religious order in India while his two other ones went to boarding schools, as did his sisters. He himself opted to become a day pupil at the local College of St. Mary's-on-the-Hill. This was a private fee-paying school run by the Christian Brothers. There were sixty pupils and four teachers. Two of these, Brothers Kane and Egan, he remembers with particular affection. They gave him a grounding both in education and life's values. The individual attention the pupils received also bore dividends. Many of his classmates went on to make their mark in society. A pupil in the year ahead of him, Jim Traynor, became a Supreme Court Judge in Hong Kong. Another one became a medical officer in the Irish Army.

There was a lot of attention to sport. There was a tennis court, a handball alley and a gym. Captain White was the athletic director. Malachy became captain of the college football team and also won a gold medal for being the best all-round athlete.

What he admired most about the school was the fact that it embodied Newman's idea of a broad education and yet wasn't intrusive. In many ways the pupils were left to their own devices. He felt himself part of a large, well-oiled machine.

Muriel Spark, who wrote *The Prime of Miss Jean Brodie*, once said: 'To me, education is a leading out of what is already there in the pupil's mind.' The Latin verb 'educare', of course, means 'leading out' so she wasn't saying anything sensationally original there, but in the early years of the last century the idea of a 'progressive' education was far into the future so St. Mary's-on-the Hill was pioneering in that regard. The fact that it had the luxury of small numbers – there were only 14 in his class – no doubt helped.

It was also pioneering, he felt, in its prioritisation of sport. This was sweet music to him. A healthy body meant a healthy mind. After a game of tennis or some circuit training his mind felt crystal clear.

His athletic prowess he put down to the fact that he had an extra lumbar vertebra, which gave him a more flexible spine. He also had long arms, a boon to any sportsman. One afternoon while playing football, however, he injured his right knee. He was in great pain and couldn't straighten it. This simple incident he regards as another catalyst for him becoming a doctor. He'd always been fascinated with pain and its alleviation, so where better to start an analysis of it than with oneself?

3

Malachy realised to his chagrin that he was going to have to pass eight exams to get into medical school, two of these being at St. Mary's. Places in medical school were at a premium and the competition to get in was fairly cut-throat. But he knuckled down and came through.

He was 18 years of age when he entered the medical faculty at UCD. How many would stick the pace? No one knew. There were always drop-outs, people who changed their minds, who couldn't stand the hard graft. He hoped he wouldn't be one of these. He had a burning ambition inside him but he was young. Was it youthful idealism that would pass as soon as he saw his first grisly patient? His sporting career had been cut off at the knees. Maybe this one would be too.

Not all of the students were models of hygiene. The toilet floor was often found flooded. This led to Malachy and his friends putting up a notice on it saying: 'We aim to please – you aim too, please'. Another notice said: 'Customers using this bank are requested not to leave small change on the counter'. A third one went, 'There's no use standing on the seat: our crabs jump six feet'.

He joined the group organising the annual 'Rag'. This was a re-enactment of the Middle Ages where there was a rivalry between the university and the town: 'Town Versus Gown'. The Gown looked down on the Town and demonstrated this by disrupting its services. He was given the job of upsetting the trains, a task he undertook with some relish. He changed the directions so that he had the trams going to the city centre labelled 'Donnybrook' instead. The conductor thwarted his plan in the end, but he'd made his iconoclastic gesture as required.

There were the usual end-of-term japes, like throwing flour over one another and so on, but nothing more ominous than that. Student doctors, unlike rock & roll stars, don't tend to throw TV sets out of windows or fill hotel baths with jelly and let it harden. (In fact student doctors don't usually stay in hotels.) It was a simpler time.

At the end of one term he remembers going to a ball with a girl and then walking all the way back to Vincent's Hospital with her at 3 a.m. In those days you didn't worry about being mugged or stabbed. Neither was the price of a drink a problem: it was a whopping sixpence for a pint of Guinness. Another girl ditched him because he wasn't a good enough dancer for her. (Obviously he hadn't partaken of enough of the Black Stuff.)

In his first year he studied subjects he had already done at St. Mary's: Chemistry, Physics, Botany and Zoology – dull stuff medical students like himself regarded as beneath them. Afterwards matters became much more specialised.

Long nights were spent poring over arcane text-books which would have little relevance to anything he would encounter during all his years of practice. It seemed as if the body was the most complex machine in creation and he was expected to become familiar with every square inch of it as well as every microbe and virus that could assail it. While others of his age group were out dating women or honing their rugby skills he burned the midnight oil.

Nobody knew what would 'come up' unless they had a crystal ball but he didn't like the idea of failure. He felt he definitely had a vocation for medicine but you couldn't be human without the hard grind wearing you down sometimes. He longed for the day he could put a plate outside his door with his name on it, a day when he wouldn't be answerable to any lecturer or consultant, when diagnoses would be down to his own gut instinct. Would he be able to survive on his own without these safety nets? He needed his wings, but every form of independence brought risks.

The more he read, it seemed, the less he knew. The body was like an undiscovered continent with too many countries to mention, and cities within those countries, and towns outside the cities, and villages outside the towns. Or maybe rivers and tributaries would have been a better analogy. The heart pumped blood through those tributaries and surrounding them were the thousand natural shocks that flesh is heir to. How could he learn them all? One would have had to be a monk – or a genius. It certainly seemed to require a photographic memory.

Sometimes you had to turn off completely, to stop reading, stop overloading your mind or all would be lost. It wasn't that all work and no play made Jack a dull boy, but rather a forgetful one. The secret was balance. You had to wind yourself up and then wind down again before the next hurdle. And keep your belief in the fact that these interconnecting tissues were actually attached to people, not exhibits in a laboratory.

The professors didn't suffer fools – or lackeys. They didn't regard it as their function to encourage their students. It was taken as read that the innate pull towards the medical life was there and didn't need to be pandered to. There would be no icing on the cake. Indeed, at times it was even hard to see the cake.

Lecture, eat, study, sleep. Lecture, eat, study, sleep. Sometimes you didn't know what day it was. The world outside might well have been Africa. How far away now did the hills of Monaghan seem. His family too. Even sport. He squeezed the latter in when and where he could – there was the balance again – but it was impossible to clear your mind completely from clutter.

He was on the first rugby team and played in the Hospital Cup for St. Vincent's. He also got a 'Varsity Blue' in the 20 yard hurdles. The coach at Belfield told him his style was completely wrong, that he was taking too many strides between the hurdles. 'You have to glide slowly over them,' he said, 'with your leading heel almost touching the crossbar.' It was good advice. No longer did he do the 'High Jump' over the hurdles. He ended up winning his heat. His mother 'watched' the race on the radio, beaming with pride as news of his victory came through.

Dating girls wasn't encouraged. This was the age when men and women sat on opposite sides of churches, where kissing couples were beaten out of bushes with blackthorn sticks. 'A crude form of contraception', as Malachy describes it. Outside a confessional once he heard thuds and burps as an embarrassed penitent was berated by a vigorous confessor in *sotto voce*. The box appeared to shake to its very foundations as the penance was administered. A regular fire-and-brimstone merchant. This was not a man to take kindly to the writhing bodies on the canal. (When Dublin Corporation considered cutting down the trees here, Malachy thought of Oliver St. John Gogarty's observation that the selfsame trees were 'more sinned against than sinning.')

He prayed for the necessary belief in himself to pull him through, but he also knew such belief really only came with experience. You wouldn't know how good – or bad – you were until you were blooded in the fray.

The first major challenge occurred in the second year as he was led into the dissecting room, a long enclosure with a central aisle and a row of tables upon which lay dead bodies. These were the bodies he was going to spend a year taking apart for surgical purposes. They reeked of Formalin. Six or seven students changed their careers at the precise moment of entering this chamber of horrors. As well as working on human bodies he also dissected various animal cadavers under the tutelage of Maureen De Valera, his co-director.

The lecturers ran a tight ship. One day a student brought in a heavy metal ball and proceeded to roll it down the steps from where he sat to the floor where the lecturer stood. It descended with a heavy thumping sound. When it reached the ground the professor in question lifted it up, walked up the steps with it and stopped at the tenth step. He then turned to the student sitting at the edge of this row and said, 'You're the culprit. Please leave the theatre'. He had counted the bumps and deduced that the perpetrator would have to be sitting in the tenth row. He got a clap as a result. (Perhaps this lecturer might have found an even more lucrative career as a detective).

Meanwhile the study went on. Interminably, it appeared to him. His mind was like a cauldron of symptoms and cures, parts of the body learned off in a dead language and cadavers dissected like peas in a pod. When, if ever, would it all become relevant? He shelved away all the data in the dusty attic of his mind to be regurgitated at will. He would meet patients and they would ring bells and press buttons in that attic – if he was lucky. Some of them would have misleading symptoms. or, even worse, none at all. In such cases he would have to try to be Sherlock Holmes as well as Hippocrates. Nothing would be simple, and Murphy's Law would rear its ugly head whenever it got the chance. Pains would appear and disappear in the unlikeliest of places, and those who possessed them would perhaps be as poor at describing them as he would be at trying to remove them.

Maybe he would be a disaster. Maybe he would freeze like a novice actor on the opening night of a play. Would nerves get the better of him? Would he realise after all his sweat that this wasn't to be his calling after all? That was the 64-marker. All he could do was hold his nose and dive into that big black hole of suffering that seemed to be the world's only constant. He might never learn the meaning of it but with the help of God – or Lady Luck – he might be able to reduce it. At this point in time he had no greater dreams than this for himself.

Malachy lived in 'digs' near the university where he savoured the freedom of life outside the groves of academe. Across the corridor from him was a fellow student called Ned Wilcox. They often walked to lectures together but Wilcox didn't have his heart in them. He liked the *idea* of being a doctor, but hardly the donkeywork involved in actually becoming one.

He also had a mischievous streak. Some days he turned up at lectures waving half-dissected dogfish and worms at the lecturer's podium. He was something of a spendthrift too, and liked to gamble on horses. Like most gamblers he always felt that one day he'd strike it rich. But the horses he followed followed the horses. The other students had a joke about him: 'Ned backed a horse at twenty to one … and it came in at half-past two.'

He pawned a lot of his clothes in a shop in Cuffe Street where he claimed to have secured good terms with the proprietor. Some of his stratagems here exhibited great ingenuity. He left his heavy winter coat in during the summer and redeemed it when the cold weather started to bite. His logic was that the said coat would last longer because it would have been worn less.

Ned also brought his gambler's temperament to his study – or rather lack of study. He tried to predict what would 'come up' in exam papers just as he tried to predict what horse would win a race. Amazingly, he passed two exams using this crystal ball technique. Obviously medical examiners were more reliable than the nags.

At the end of Malachy's second year he found Ned pacing around the Convocation Hall like an expectant father as all of the students waited for the results of their exams. Maybe he twigged that the jig was finally up for him because he said, 'Let's go down to University Church and light a few candles.' Malachy felt this smacked of desperation but agreed to accompany his caddish friend. When they got to the church Ned took two pennies from his pocket and lit two candles.

When they got back to the hall they looked up who had passed. Under S, Malachy spotted his own name as one of the lucky ones but there was nothing under W for Ned. The candles, evidently, hadn't done the trick. Or maybe God felt he needed to be taught a lesson.

'Let's go back to the church,' said Ned in a fit of pique. Malachy shrugged his shoulders, wondering what was coming next. When they got there the two unhelpful candles were half-burned out. Ned stubbed the last flickers out of them and put them in his pocket as he strode from the church. Malachy expected him to blow a cylinder head gasket but the opposite happened.

'Somebody is trying to tell me something,' he said, remembering Oscar Wilde's dictum 'When the Gods wish to punish us, they answer our prayers.'

Ned cleaned up his act, put his head into the books and became a model student. It looked like the candles had done their job after all, by waking him up to the fact that there are no short-cuts in life.

He gave up the horses and the pawnshops and acquired patience. And patients.

4

The last two years of Malachy's medical training upped the ante of laboratory work and he also had to spend three months in a maternity hospital.

It was intoxicating walking down the ward on his first day. Excitement mixed with insecurity made the contact with his initial patient acquire added dimensions. An ingrown toenail would have been treated with the same *gravitas* as a quadruple bypass. Going out into the firing line after all that theorising was a different kind of test. As in every business, a doctor needed customers. There would always be sickness, so the medical profession would never become defunct, but some doctors obviously had more thriving practices than others. And it wasn't all down to *savoir faire*. The clichéd phrase 'bedside manner' only scratched the surface. Maybe one needed to be something of a psychologist as well as a diagnostician, or PR man. No two patients were alike. Little did those early patients realise that, if truth were told, he was actually more nervous than they were.

His maternity hospital contract entailed assisting at a baby's delivery. He wasn't a total novice to the reproduction process at this point of his life, having been present when a cow calved on a farm in Monaghan. (The cow, as he remembered, took it all with a phlegmatic interest.) He had also, while bird-nesting as a child, let a chicken out of an egg. When he removed the shell the chicken had stretched itself, jumped up and moved away. It all seemed delightfully simple.

There were three students with him on the day he witnessed his first human delivery. As well as the woman about to give birth, there was also an obstetrician present, and an anaesthetist. A nurse stood by the patient, exhorting her to bear down. Malachy positioned himself at the side of the bed with his colleagues, rigid with excitement. Suddenly the woman said she felt a strong pain coming on.

'Good,' said the nurse.

'No,' said the woman, 'It's bad, very bad.'

'Bear down,' said the doctor, 'bear down really hard.'

She did as she was bidden and after a good heave, a white rounded creature appeared between her legs. The head slithered out slowly and then Malachy saw a face amid a torrent of fluid and blood as well as mucus. Finally, a fully-formed baby was positioned in the arms of the obstetrician, followed by a long white cord like a hose running to a house in a fire.

The baby started sputtering and coughing then, and the doctor cried out 'Get the suction going.' At this point, one of Malachy's more squeamish colleagues slipped to the floor in a faint. Malachy looked at the woman and she winked at him, leading him to believe another pregnancy could be on the cards if she fancied him. (In that case, he could be present at the conception as well as the delivery!)

As part of his training he had to deliver a baby in the mother's home. Home births are of course an extreme rarity now but they were common when he was young. An ambulance was on standby in case something went wrong. If there were less serious complications, some more experienced doctors were called out to assist.

Since the hospital he worked in was in Ringsend, this was also the area allotted to him for his groundbreaking task. He was given the address and strode manfully out into the night armed with his black bag and some instruments.

The woman in question already had twelve children. When he reached her house an urchin ran up some worn wooden stairs beside it crying out 'Ma, the doctor is here.' He followed him up and entered a small room with a large bed in the centre. The woman about to give birth was sitting in it smoking a cigarette. 'Hello doc,' she said. 'How are you?' he asked. 'I'll soon be all right,' she replied. He took this as a vote of confidence.

A nurse was standing by. Beside her was a chest of drawers and a large washbasin with a water jug on it. In the next room he could hear laughing and loud guffaws. A tiny fire flickered in a small grate and he thought: The stage is set.

The woman cried out in sudden pain then and the nurse stripped down the sheets. He tried to remember all his training and brought the baby forth with the same gush of liquid as before. At this point the babble of voices from next door grew louder. The woman who'd given birth said, 'That was quick. You're a good doctor. What's your name?' 'Malachy Smyth,' he said, whereupon the woman said, 'Let's call the baby Malachy.' And she did. (He afterwards learned that Malachy is a very common name around Ringsend to this day.)

The nurse picked up the afterbirth and threw it into the fire. It almost went out as a result, but then flared up into a smoky yellow flame. He picked up his black bag and headed back to the hospital, mission accomplished.

After the maternity hospital it was nothing but books, lectures and the dissecting-room. By now he had become philosophical about the latter. We need dead people to keep the living alive, he told himself.

It wasn't all solemnity, however. He was working in a London hospital one Christmas and the resident nurse informed him there was going to be some entertainment. It turned out to be a comedian with a performing flea. The flea, called Freda, jumped upon command and landed on the comedian's hand. It also performed a backward flip and a double back somersault. It was reluctant to do the latter (because of fears for its spine?) but agreed in the end, having been persuaded in 'flea language'. Tragedy struck when 'Freda' disappeared towards the end of the act ... and was eventually found on the lapel of the hospital matron's coat. Or so he thought. Having coaxed it onto his finger he carefully examined it and exclaimed in horror: 'This is not my flea!' Exit one underwhelmed matron.

As Malachy's final exams approached, eyes that had withstood the grim sight of cadavers without a by-your-leave now started to water. Palms sweated profusely and deals were made with the Almighty: 'Pull me through this, Lord, and I'll never skip another lecture – or 'borrow' anyone else's stethoscope without giving it back.' One roll of the dice meant the difference between moving on to the next level or going back to square one, as Ned Wilcox had experienced.

He knew the money wasn't there for that. The days crawled by as all sorts of thoughts went through his mind. What if he got an examiner who didn't like him for one reason or another and had his sights set on failing him? What if a condition he was asked to treat in the practicals just happened to be his Achilles heel? It was common knowledge that interns seized up when put on the spot. It was like an actor 'corpsing' – an unimaginable thought. He banished it from his mind. Some nights, he knew, it was important to lay off. That's where sport came to his rescue. After a game of rugby everything seemed clearer, more simple. He could treat the Pope without getting the jitters. But then night-time came again, and the apprehensiveness. He just wanted it to be over.

And then one day it was. He passed. He was now Doctor Smyth. All of the work had finally been worth it.

Only 35 of his class lasted the pace: exactly half the original number. Some opted for different careers, some failed their exams and some even died. One student was 'sent down' for stealing his overcoat. He had hung it on the rack in the College of Science one day on his way into the lecture hall and when he came back it was gone. It was subsequently pawned and the gardaí traced it to the pawnshop in question. Malachy identified it in court. To his relief, Ned Wilcox hadn't been the culprit.

And now the future loomed. What did it hold for him? Would he be able to stay in Ireland or would he have to emigrate to find work?

History itself was about to make the decision for him.

5

When the British declared war on Germany on September 3, 1939 it was done in muted fashion. Gone was the jingoism of August 1914 when it found itself in a similar predicament. The legacy of memories from World War I bit too hard into the collective gut for that. Practically every family in the country knew somebody who had been killed in that war and they feared history would repeat itself now that Hitler was on the march again. Nonetheless, there was no alternative. In March of 1939 Britain, along with France, pledged to defend Belgium, Holland and Poland against attack by the Fuhrer.

On September 1 Hitler attacked Poland and two days later the process of mobilisation began. Rearmament was accelerated, air-raid shelters built and gas masks distributed. There was no going back now.

This wasn't the way Hitler had planned it. He imagined that if he conquered France, Britain would cede Europe to Germany. He didn't think that the British, who had racial ties with his own country, would be so keen to 'have a crack at jerry'.

Malachy qualified as a doctor just as World War II was beginning. Maybe active service at the front would have been the easier option as things worked out.

He got a job as a House Physician in the Royal Devon and Exeter hospital in Exeter. This was a short-time post of six months, designed to help him learn the rudiments of medical practice. He lived in the hospital and was on duty from dawn to dusk. There was a continuous stream of patients with a tremendous variety of complaints – everything from cut fingers to major abdominal injuries. He'd never worked before and now here he was being thrown in at the deep end in this strange building.

Outside in the greater world, the war reached fever-pitch. Panic was rife. People were drilling into the ground with spades and farm implements as they built shelters for themselves. An invasion was expected at any moment.

Patients came in sporadically at first, mainly as a result of U-boat activities at sea, but then after three months the bombing of a ship in the English Channel resulted in 150 casualties suddenly arriving at the hospital. Many soldiers were maimed beyond recognition. He gritted his teeth and prepared them for surgery. Sometimes he thought he was going to lose his breakfast but he was moving so fast he didn't have time to be properly shocked. Mortars were exploding everywhere, making the floors he walked on vibrate. It was like being in the middle of an earthquake, albeit one caused by man. The hospital itself had also been bombed, Exeter being just across the Channel from France. There were only twelve doctors there, even though it had 400 beds available. Many of the younger doctors had been called up to the Armed Forces so there was a serious shortage. Malachy had sixty patients under him and was informed be was the hospital's resident anaesthetist. As somebody who had only administered three short anaesthetics before this point in time, this was something of a baptism of fire.

Because the war had thinned the ranks he agreed to this zany state of affairs, but then things started happening too fast. One day a German fighter plane was shot down over the city. The pilot baled out and was captured, afterwards being admitted to the hospital because of a severe wound in his hand which had to be surgically repaired. As the only anaesthetist in the hospital, the task fell to Malachy.

The pilot arrived in on a trolley being wheeled by a nurse. He was clearly terrified. He told Malachy he'd been warned in Germany that he would be tortured if captured alive in England. Malachy told him this was nonsense but he remained unconvinced.

He was reminded of the comment of Winston Churchill: 'A prisoner of war is a man who tries to kill you and fails, and then asks you not to kill him.'

He started to administer the ether and chloroform to the pilot but he didn't want it. He roared like a man possessed, refusing to go under. He started to flail at everything with his fists and leapt off the operating table in a frenzy. He then made a bolt for the door. Malachy gave chase.

He wasn't unaware of the absurdity of the situation. What was he to do? Call out, 'Stop or I'll stab you'? (In military parlance, his surgical syringe could double as a bayonet). In actual fact he caught up with the blessed soldier and knocked him to the floor with a flying tackle, using all of his UCD experience. (Somehow, he couldn't remember the necessity of rugby tackles being recommended for captured German pilots in any of his medical textbooks.)

By now the nurse had also become involved in the melée and was entangled in the legs of both doctor and patient, making a rather curious trio. Next door, meanwhile, the surgeon who was going to perform the operation – a retired man known affectionately as Colonel Blimp – heard the tumult outside and began to suspect the worst. Maybe he thought the damage done to the poor pilot's hand was being exacerbated by those employed to treat it.

Malachy could imagine a speculative conversation between himself and the surgeon, whereby the surgeon asked him if the patient was etherised yet and Malachy replied that he was, and would be ready for his operation as soon as his gattling gun ran out of ammo.

'What the hell is going on here?' he shouted out, charging through the swing door.

'The prisoner tried to escape.' Malachy informed him as he picked himself and his reluctant patient up off the floor.

'Jolly good show, Smyth old boy,' Colonel Blimp offered, 'Jolly good. Only for you the bastard would have got away.' Perhaps there was a note of irony in the tone, but Malachy took the comment at face value. The pilot was immediately replaced on the table and the necessary surgery was performed on him without the necessity for any more rugby tackles on the part of the rookie doctor.

6

Dr Smyth's anaesthetic career, if such it could be called, had come to an abrupt end, but if he imagined tranquillity was to follow he had another think coming because he was now called up for RAF service. Before he knew what was happening he was sent to a training centre in Sidmonton, Devon. He was promptly informed he was no longer a civilian as he donned the army uniform.

There were fifteen doctors here and they were put through the routines of military life, being taught how to salute and march and so on. Some of the older ones understandably saw this as ridiculous.

They were all posted to RAF stations throughout the country as 'flying officers'. Malachy ended up in Sussex, becoming doctor to a night-fighting squadron defending London. This squadron had 'mosquito' planes which flew at about 500 mph. They were armed with 20mm Cannon in each wing. They also had radar and a radio operator, making them sophisticated for their time. The radio operator was informed from Ground Control as to the whereabouts of German bomber planes. He could see such planes as blips on his radar screen, which gave him an advantage the Nazis didn't have. Malachy likened the latter's beleaguered predicament to that of fish swimming in shark-infested waters. They were seen without being able to see back, a nightmare scenario for any soldier.

In the nether regions of the upper night sky you fired at a flash or a white cloud if it seemed to move, or was in the right place. It was like firing at the tail of a deer as it jumped into a thicket in a deer hunt. In gladiatorial tussles no quarter was asked and none was given. Victory always went to the quickest finger. The fighter plane was aptly named after the mosquito. With its radar eye it could dart in undetected and then sting and vanish.

The squadron was divided into two flight sections, with a wing commander over both. They did two nights on duty, each flight alternating. Between flights they lay ensconced in dispersal huts camouflaged on the edge of the runway. The aeroplanes, meanwhile, cowered in bays outside, armed for action. Inside the huts pilots lounged around in armchairs, some of them reading, some snoozing, some smoking. They were all dressed for immediate flight, which included having to wear oxygen masks. Such masks weren't available in the old days, causing many pilots to become de-oxygenated as they soared up too quickly in the air, resulting in them losing consciousness and plunging to their death in a matter of moments before battle commenced at all.

To test the efficacy of such masks, Malachy volunteered to enter a decompression chamber shortly after he began training. He went in with a friend and was seated at a bench, a table in front of him. The pair of them were given a pencil and paper and told to write their names and other details about themselves, the instructions coming from outside via a telephone. As soon as he started writing the pressure of the oxygen reduced so quickly that he lost consciousness. So did his friend. When he woke up a minute later he saw that he hadn't even completed writing his name.

As a result of experiences like this he felt he was as close to being a soldier as could be. He thought of it as being similar to being in the butts waiting for a covey of pheasants to appear - except that these pheasants shot back. If a pilot crashed on landing he rushed to the spot. Occasionally he could help but usually the pilot in question was dead.

In some instances it fell to him to give the wife of the dead pilot her husband's uniform, and his wedding ring. There were even incidents where a man's hand might have been blown off as he crashed to the ground and the ring in question had to be looked for and prised off a severed hand. One needed a strong stomach for such times.

He came close to death one night himself when a landing strip 100 yards away from him was raked by machine gun fire. It could have been him. The roulette wheel spun and one day it landed on your number and you were shot down and killed. Afterwards you were decorated and talked about as a war hero. But what good was that to your widow and children? You couldn't hug a memory, even a heroic one. Medals were only reminders of what wasn't there.

The pilots were watched constantly by Ground Control as the aerial cat-and-mouse game went on. If they didn't come up to expectations, or press home their initiative, they could be charged with 'lack of moral fibre'. This was a very serious offence which might even result in a court martial and dismissal from the forces with dishonour. This was extremely rare, however, and most pilots were decorated for bravery with an Air Force cross.

The expression 'lack of moral fibre' (LMF) was a euphemism for cowardice, as he was well aware. It meant that you were 'letting the side down', betraying the *esprit de corps*. A stiff upper lip had to be preserved at all times, even if one was a shivering jelly inside. In the hospital he saw some beds actually shaking from the trembling of soldiers who had come close to death. Many of them were praying. If there were no atheists in the foxholes, as the saying went, neither were there any in hospital beds.

Some soldiers, over-wrought with fear, returned from missions prematurely with, quote unquote, 'technical' problems. Eyebrows were raised at this by the MO in charge. A commanding officer might see it as desertion under another name. He might wish to make an example of the pilot in charge, fearing such an excuse, or alibi, might be taken up by others in the squadron. This, remember, was an age long before soldiers in the Vietnam war burned their draft cards in Main Street as 'conscientious objectors'. In the forties, 'the cause' was still an ideal.

If a soldier was deemed to be 'guilty' of LFM he was sometimes arrested before being interviewed by a psychiatrist. The psychiatrist in question might use a form of bribery to try and entice him back to the front, informing him that if he didn't go he would lose whatever stripes he had and be transferred to some other division where his name would be mud. His duties here would be so menial as to be degrading. His history would also become common knowledge to others in the camp, making the stigma all the worse.

Though this was still preferable to the treatment meted out to soldiers in similar circumstances in World War I - these were often put up against a wall and shot by firing squad, with their widows even being refused a pension - many of them succumbed to the bribery and dragged themselves back to the front, fearing the ignominy of their threatened demotion almost more than death from the enemy. Many such soldiers went back to their places and promptly got shot down due to their judgment being impaired from the fear. Others performed reckless acts which were mistakenly seen as heroic. Desperation would have been a more apt term.

The lesser of many evils would have been to come back wounded. One's pride could be preserved then, and also one's life. If the wound was bad enough it would be unlikely the soldier in question would see any more action.

Some soldiers experienced huge pangs of guilt as a result of not feeling able to face the trenches again. Instead of professional treatment they got little more than tea and sympathy. The stiff upper lip had to be preserved at all times. These men may have seen their best friends blown to pieces by a shell or landmine mere inches away and were expected to take it in their stride. Nobody told them that *not* to have an over-wrought reaction to this state would have been the abnormality. Only robots, or people whose perception of war didn't go beyond Errol Flynn movies, would fail to realise this. But sadly a lot of 'analysts' could be numbered in either category.

Whenever a pilot was in danger of being charged with dereliction of duty, Malachy would summon him to the sick quarter. More often than not he would find a medical reason for his behaviour and manage to get him transferred from flying to an administrative post. No fingers were pointed at anyone as a result and brave men who couldn't perform as they might have liked to – for any number of reasons - weren't crucified by the system.

At times it all seemed like Joseph Heller's classic case of Catch-22, the stipulation whereby a pilot got out of bombing missions by claiming he was insane … but how could he be insane if he wanted to get out of bombing missions?

Some men did go insane during this war, having been humiliated before they tipped over the edge. In today's age, what with all of the research into post-traumatic stress syndrome and the like, such conditions are diagnosed with a degree more sophistication but this was the war where General George Patton slapped a shellshocked soldier and then delivered this diatribe to him: 'Shut up that goddam crying. I won't have brave men here seeing a yellow bastard like you bawling. You're going back to the frontlines and you may get shot or killed, but you're going to fight. If you don't, I'll stand you up against a wall and have a firing squad kill you. I ought to do it myself, you whimpering coward.'

Many people now believe that Patton himself was suffering from battle fatigue. A week after this incident, at a different hospital, he punched another soldier in the head and threatened to shoot him as well. As a result of the second incident he lost his command and had to make a public apology. The ironic upshot of all of this was that he actually made the military more aware than ever of the catastrophic effects of shellshock on the mind. 'Old Blood and Guts' may have done more for psychiatric research than liberal souls campaigning endlessly for more understanding of distraught veterans.

'War makes men barbarous,' Cesare Pavese wrote, 'because to take part in it one must harden oneself against all regret, all appreciation of delicacy and sensitive values. One must live as if those values did not exist, and when the war is over one has lost the resilience to return to those values.' The quote took on added repercussions for the battle-scarred.

It should also be stressed that shellshock wasn't just confined to soldiers. Thousands of civilians suffered from panic attacks and other neuroses at this time as a result of the war, which meant that hospital wards in all the main cities were swollen with patients who never donned a uniform.

Some soldiers came into the hospital suffering from paralysis but no medical explanation could be found. Others had nightmares, hallucinations, amnesia, loss of speech and blindness. The lion's share of these men were suffering some form of nervous disorder. A tiny percentage, of course, were manufacturing symptoms to avoid having been sent back to the front, or to get themselves a military pension, but most of them were deranged from being in the thick of the action. Some even became schizophrenic, and/or suicidal. Many developed psychosomatic illnesses.

In a simpler age than our own such illnesses were rarely diagnosed accurately. Some patients were hypnotised to 'put them right'. In chronic cases, a rudimentary form of ECT was used, which often exacerbated the condition. A frontal lobotomy was a last resort. One doctor pioneered a system of 'deep sleep' treatment which had a limited degree of success. Others opted for the innocuous and rather irrelevant Group Therapy, a fad then in its infancy. The one thing a soldier knew for sure was that if he expressed any reluctance to continue to serve his country he would be regarded as a blemish on his regiment, and the scar would be permanent.

Psychiatry was the Cinderella of medicine during the war years. The thinking was, 'Have a few sedatives and you'll be fine.' It didn't go any deeper than that at the time. Or maybe it didn't want to. Maybe the authorities felt if they adopted a 'softly softly' approach it might lead to large numbers of disenchanted (or lily-livered) soldiers looking for a shortcut back to Civvy Street.

There were very few of these, in Malachy's view. The soldiers he saw were too dumbstruck to be this canny. Their main frame of mind was bewilderment. They might have known what they were fighting *against* – the Nazis – but not many of them were aware of what they were fighting *for*.

Some soldiers had 'out of body' experiences as a result of shellshock. Ernest Hemingway, who was wounded in World War 1, described the experience of being hit by shrapnel as being similar to your soul leaving your body. He acted blasé about it after it happened but some interpreters of his work and life contend that he suffered a lifelong neurosis as a result of this. Malachy met like-minded soldiers who had suppressed their shock, or sublimated it.

After Hemingway was injured he said he was surrounded by so many dead bodies that dying seemed a more natural and normal thing than to survive. For a time he even considered shooting himself with his officer's pistol – an ironic reaction considering he would indeed shoot himself some forty years on.

Malachy looked into the eyes of the soldiers brought in to him for signs of dementia. Many of them just gazed blankly into the middle distance,

31

unable or unwilling to answer even the most basic questions. Some of them would have limbs amputated, others would carry residual pain with them to their dying day.

The problems of others were harder to pin down. Though bearing no physical scars, they were palpably distraught. What terrors lurked inside those handsome features? What agonies had gone through their heads before they were shot down, just at the moment of impact? As they were dragged from their planes, what fate did they imagine awaited them?

His qualification wasn't psychiatry so he could merely wonder how they would fare as they lay there going through preliminary tests for concussion before being handed over to higher authorities. An automatic instinct made him deduce that many of them were in worse circumstances than those who had parts of their arms or legs blown off. You could get a prosthetic arm but what could you get for your brain? Was their any pill that would banish the demons from one's skull a month or year or decade hence when memories of that moment of impact started to haunt them?

They might be settled down in the suburbs with a wife and children and performing some trivial task at work or home when it all came alive for them again and they re-lived that moment in all its brutish horror, the banished memories rising up from the subconscious to make the war a happening thing again, as graphic and vivid as when it was taking place in real time.

Would they be able to share their fears with their loved ones or elect to hide them in case they disturbed whatever dubious domestic harmony they had created in the interim? Would such protective camouflage – the psychological equivalent of the battle fatigues they wore to help them merge into the surrounding terrain – in the end prove more counter-productive than a full declaration that all was not right? Only those well on the way to civilian readjustment might be able to come clean in such circumstances.

Others would bottle up their frustrations, thereby creating an emotional block that would seek some other form of release in time. For some, that release could come at a huge price. They might even choose suicide as an out.

A poet called Gunner McPhail put it succinctly:

Perhaps you're broke and paralysed
Perhaps your memory goes
But it's only just called shell-shock
For you've nothing there that shows.

As a result of the myopic psychiatric mindset, such patients were regarded

The young Malachy (right) training at Belfield U.C.D.

Malachy (left) and friend take a breather

The doctor with an old war aeroplane which was being dismantled at a depot in the Sahara Desert.

At the Royal Infirmary, Edinburgh.

IN THE SAHARA DESERT

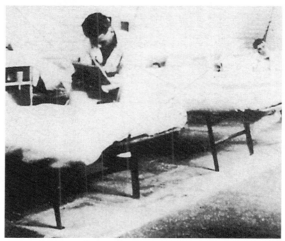

Sick quarters - sometimes German prisoners were the patients.

An encampment. One had to be careful not to walk barefoot here as scorpions lurked in the fine sand. A nip on the sole of the foot often caused temporary paralysis of the legs.

Pope Pius XII, whose fears Malachy allayed towards the end of World War II

Field Marshal Rommel leading by example

Dr. Malachy and Lucy on their wedding day,
with Malachy's brother Declan, who married them.

Lucy in the gardens of a clinic in Florence.

Dr. Malachy's cousin Marie Smith (left)
and a friend in Monterey, California.

RICHARD NIXON
WASHINGTON, D. C.

November 1, 1968

Dr. M. J. Smyth
1611 Genesee St.
Utica, New York 13501

Dear Dr. Smyth:

   I want to express my personal appreciation for your efforts on behalf of my
candidacy for President of the United States.

   Only a few hours remain before the
future of our country will be settled at the
polls on Tuesday, November 5th.

   We have thus far succeeded, but I can
be elected only with your further help. So
now, Dr. Smyth, I ask if you will please do
this: on Election Day will you persuade at
least four of your friends and neighbors in
Utica who share our goals to cast their
ballots for our ticket.

   This is the final and most important
step in our campaign. We will win if you and
others personally volunteer to get our
supporters to the voting booths.

   My warmest thanks for your help as we
move forward to victory.

                          Sincerely,

                          Richard Nixon

Richard Nixon, an unlikely cash cow for Dr. Malachy, shaking hands
with John F. Kennedy

Dr. Malachy's house in Utica

The doctor on Keuka Lake, one of the Finger Lakes
in upper New York State

Dr. Malachy (left, seated) with relatives in Monterey, California

Dr. Malachy's cousin James F. Smith (front, centre) during the Spanish-American War in the Philippines in 1908

An Apology to a Distinguished
Orthopedic Surgeon:

MALACHY JOSEPH SMYTH, M.D., F.A.C.S., F.R.C.S.

The Classic article entitled "Sciatica and the Intervertebral Disk," published in Volume 129, was written by M. J. Smyth and V. J. Wright. M. J. Smyth is Malachy Joseph Smyth of Utica, New York, who is very much alive, and not Michael Joseph Smyth 1892–1964, whose photograph, through an error of mistaken identity, appears on page 10 of Volume 129.

Fig.1 Malachy Joseph Smyth. 1919-

Malachy Joseph Smyth, M.D., F.A.C.S., F.R.C.S., qualified in 1939 as a physician in the Medical School of University College, Dublin. During World War II he served in the Royal Air Force in England, the Middle East, and Italy. Later he became a Senior Fellow in Orthopaedics, working full time in the University Hospital, Leeds, and the Royal Infirmary, Hull, England. In 1958, after 5 years of research on experimental and clinical sciatica, Malachy J. Smith published "Sciatica and the Intervertebral Disk" with Verna Wright as coauthor. In 1959 he was awarded both a Traveling Fellowship to Italy and a research award by the Leeds Regional Hospital Board. In 1960 Dr. Smyth accepted a post as Clinical Research Fellow in Toronto, and in 1962 he established a private orthopedic practice in New York State where he continues to work.

M.R.U.

The mistaken identity apology

A caricature by Lucy of James O'Brien, a judge friend, made to look fearsome.

Dr. Malachy on a golfing holiday in Sea Island, Georgia.

A medieval banquet in Dromoland Castle. Left to right: Dr. Malachy, Lucy, Doris and Dr. T. Kantor

Clambake at Newport, Rhode Island. Left: Dr. Malachy. Right: Dr Grady, an orthopedic surgeon from Boston

The doctor in 1994

either as cowards or psychotic; there was no in-between. After a rudimentary 'cure' being administered for their condition, they were then sent back to the mortar and the madness, which was a bit like 'curing' a victim of sexual abuse by sending him back to a paedophile.

As time went on, thankfully, the hero-coward dichotomy gave way to a general recognition that every man was vulnerable to some degree, and anyone who had been exposed to shellfire on a consistent basis was a prime candidate for unhingement. Such men were unlikely to ever be totally normal again, no matter how many years they lived after the war. An official statement to soldiers' wives after the Battle of Dunkirk said, 'Don't worry if your man screams at night, or throws himself down when a plane flies over the back garden.' The scars of devastation lay like micro-chips in these men's heads, waiting to be downloaded by some trigger. The lucky ones were those who exhibited their terrors openly. At least that way there was some chance of coming to grips with them over time. The silent sufferers hid their discomfiture from their families and friends, and often even from themselves. Some of them failed abjectly to return to civilian life, replaying the war in their heads into old age like a film they wished to censor but couldn't.

Some soldiers even injured themselves to get out of the war, shooting themselves in the arm or foot to bring this about. If they were found to be guilty of a self-inflicted would (SIW) due to the type of bullet used, they were sent to a lunatic asylum. One was again reminded of Joe Heller. How could this be insanity when one was facing such danger on a day-to-day basis? (Others even wounded themselves before they were conscripted at all.)

The RAF top brass didn't seem to understand anything about fear, their main concern being to improve the technology at their disposal. If they had better planes they thought it was axiomatic that the fear factor would dissipate, or at least reduce itself. They concerned themselves with tangential issues like the low temperatures in the planes, which sometimes caused frostbite and chills, or the lengthy exposure to high altitudes with low pressure and lack of oxygen, as already mentioned.

No matter how highly equipped the planes were, the more missions one flew, particularly at night-time over enemy terrain, the more likely one was to be shot down. That's why it was imperative there was a ceiling placed on the number of missions a pilot was delegated to go on. There had to be some incentive, Malachy knew, some end in sight beyond one's own mortality. You had to sweeten the pill by giving rest periods between flights. It might also have been advisable for those who were giving the orders to sit in the cramped conditions the pilots were experiencing day by day and night by night, to understand the terror involved.

The unmentionable 'F' word was fear. It didn't seem to strike commanders that bravery came from overcoming it rather than not being susceptible to it. The man with nerves of steel wasn't brave; rather he was immune. The one who went out into the dark unknown in a cold sweat was infinitely more courageous.

7

It was only after the war ended that people saw it objectively. When one was in the thick of the action, as Malachy was, all he could concentrate on was the next patient, the next mortar, the next travesty.

Performing surgery in a war zone was like building a house on the edge of a cliff. The fact that the hospital itself could theoretically be bombed in the middle of the operation gave everything a surreal quality.

Surgeons sutured to the background music of gunfire, the screams of the patients piercing the night like the sounds of violins out of tune, the bombs drowning them out finally as yet another edifice was reduced to rubble in the blink of an eye.

Every building was like a loaded gun waiting to explode. Malachy could hear the silence. Measuring its length between air raid sirens was like measuring the length between the thunder and the flashes of lightning. Any moment could be one's last.

He often heard the rattle of gunfire, and then the sound of a plane going down. Soon afterwards the bodies would be wheeled in, dead or dying, young men in the prime of their lives gasping for breath as the blood oozed out of them. And for what?

The wounded from both sides were admitted in equal numbers. The uniform didn't matter. Sometimes it was unrecognisable anyway under the blood. Men who could have been friends if they'd met in peacetime had risked their lives to kill one another because of the mad dreams of a demagogue. Now they lay on operating tables beside one another fighting for their lives. It was insanity.

Some of the soldiers died even though they had been operated on successfully. This was as a result of infections picked up in Casualty. This was long before the days of Intensive Care Units or effective antibiotics. Some of the medical staff were also below par. In one operation Malachy heard about, a patient woke up in mid-surgery, having been given an insufficient anaesthetic. Another one complained of post-surgical cramps, a further operation revealing that a sponge had been left inside his body. It was so caked in blood it hadn't been noticed.

Historians would describe this as 'the last gentleman's war', but Malachy didn't see much gentlemanliness in it. If somebody had come in to his hospital stricken down with some terrible disease, he would have moved heaven and earth to try and cure them, but these were like self-inflicted wounds. A few hours before, these young men would have been in the prime of their health as they entered the cockpits of their planes. Now, because they'd taken their eye off the enemy for a milli-second they were covered in shrapnel, or had a piece of metal sticking out of them.

It wasn't a question of fixing a lumbar problem or some mysterious niggling pain. These men's entire backs were destroyed. What relevance had the study of pain relief into this? It was like putting a sticking plaster onto a cancer wound.

The sirens droned through the night like the wailing of an old dog in pain as he sat waiting for the next array of the walking wounded. Many of them were pronounced dead on arrival. The ones who weren't, an intern commented as he surveyed the blood, might have been better off if they had. But you couldn't look at it that way. He worked with what he got until there was no hope left. Outside of that all he could do was pray. In the aftermath of the sirens and the moaning, silence was indeed golden.

He watched the soldiers lying motionless on their beds, exchanging a word or two with their friends now and then but no more than that. Their scars seemed to have numbed them. He wondered in how many other wards in how many other countries similar patients lay similarly supine, confused as to why they were spared and their comrades weren't. Death was like a palpable thing in the building, a presence that cavalierly decided who would pull through and who wouldn't.

He occasionally heard a bell ringing, followed by the rush of feet that signalled a cardiac arrest or a sudden change in a patient's condition. Sometimes he know the person and sometimes he didn't. The not-knowing acted as a small balm. You couldn't give yourself to every patient or you would get dragged down by the futility of it all.

Afterwards there would be silence, the silence either of relief or tragedy. Often he wouldn't know. The dark would come down like a sheet, enveloping everyone beneath it. If he was lucky he would sleep. If not he would spend the night replaying the day's events in his mind.

He and his colleagues were trying to bring medicine into the future, while outside the hospital an almost primitive form of combat was going on. One step forward, two steps backward. Doctors boasted of being able to save people that a previous generation couldn't due to revelatory research, but military 'expertise' was also finding ways to kill people faster. A later generation would coin the term 'smart' bomb to denote one that could do less collateral damage but any idiot knew that the term 'smart bomb' was a contradiction in terms. Would the cycle ever end? Hardly. In the Bible the first son born to Adam and Eve killed his brother, thereby setting a pattern for the next 2000 years. Maybe the first doctor was murdered too.

Malachy's squadron commander was called Max Redford and he struck up a good friendship with him. After the war ended, Max said, he intended emigrating to America and taking up horse-ranching on the prairies. He was the son of a journalist, a friend of G.K. Chesterton, and more interested in writing than fighting. As indeed was Malachy.

Max strode into his sick quarters one morning and asked him if he'd like to go with him on a night-flying expedition. He had a 'gremlin' in his aircraft and wanted to make sure it was sorted out before his next mission. 'I want to throw the plane around the sky for a bit,' he said, 'and see if I can shake it off.' Malachy agreed to accompany him.

They did some aerobatics but Max still wasn't happy with the plane's performance, despite the fact that he'd been assured by the aircraft crew that was it AOK. 'It's probably just a leprechaun,' Malachy joked, 'and they're friendly.' Max smiled ruefully at this. 'Why not take a night off,' Malachy pressed, 'We could go to a show together.' He always felt Max was pushing himself too hard. But Max demurred. 'I feel I might get a bomber tonight,' he said, his eyes lighting up with excitement.

Later that night his prediction seemed about to come true because a bombing raid developed. Max had just lit a cigarette in the Dispersal Hut when the order to scramble came. Malachy watched him deposit it in an ash tray as he made his way out to be what would be his last mission. He was in the air in minutes, vectored onto an incoming German plane. He radioed Ground Control to say he had a bomber in his sights but after that there was a deafening silence.

Despite repeated efforts to contact him, there was no reply. Malachy looked at the cigarette Max had left in the ash tray. It was still lighting, a coil of blue smoke ascending from it as it burned itself down to the filter tip. Up in the sky, however, a different kind of smoke was visible…

Smoking kills, they say. But if he'd finished his cigarette he might still be alive today.

Max was shot down by a tail gunner. Nobody knew if the gremlin was to blame - or the leprechaun. Malachy now regretted his dry humour, and the fact that he hadn't pressed Max further to go to a show with him. But he doubted he would have listened, He'd always been a driven personality, driven finally beyond his limits. What had he twigged that the aircraft crew hadn't? What intuition had he that something was wrong? Nobody could put their finger on it. It was the instinct of a man who knew a plane like other people knew cars or boats. Or maybe he was just the victim of a freak hit. No matter what technology you've got, there's no answer to that.

George Bernard Shaw once said that a single death was a tragedy, a thousand a statistic. Malachy felt the full force of the tragedy that night. The following day Max would be just another subheading on a newspaper, another casualty of a war he had never wanted hand, act or part in. It had robbed him of everything; there would be no horse-ranching in the prairies now.

The words of the W.B. Yeats poem *An Irish Airman Foresees His Death* sprang to mind: 'I know that I shall meet my fate/Somewhere in the skies above.' Maybe Max had a hunch his number was up and needed to know for sure, to hasten things to their conclusion. Either that or the gremlins were in his own head.

The sky was starless. The moon shone down on the sea as the waves surged towards the shore like a different kind of invasion. Malachy watched them licking their way up the wall of the pier like giant worms of spray and thought of another line from a poem, the one that ends Matthew Arnold's *On Dover Beach*: 'Where ignorant armies clash by night.'

A week later he was asked to meet Max's wife and supervise the handing over of his belongings to her: his impeccably pressed blue uniform and other personal effects. It was a horrible task, as horrible as looking for the wedding rings of men who were blown to smithereens by men from another country who were as much victims of the whole madness as Max and Malachy were. Or anybody else who donned a uniform for the cause. Ours not to wonder why, ours but to do and die.

Meanwhile, on a hundred different night shifts in a hundred different dispersal huts, men like Max took their last drag of a cigarette before making their way out into the night and met their fate before it had burned to the tip, while men like Malachy placated their widows with lame bromides.

Generals made decisions with little sticks and maps from the comfort of their bunkers while the small Austrian megalomaniac with the toothbrush moustache continued to press onwards across Europe. The world and his wife watched and waited for loved ones to come home or not come home as a recently qualified doctor from across the pond listened to the cries of the injured from hospital wards, the war raging on in its fitful, tortuous trajectory.

8

During the following years Malachy was shuffled here and there across Europe, Africa and the Middle East. He saw pain in many forms, from the diseases endemic in the desert to the wounds caused by men forcing others to follow their lead.

He felt like he was caught in some kind of a whirlpool, being flung this way and that by unseen forces. Would his life ever come to a point where he himself was its main impetus? Would he ever see the day when he could call the shots? Nonetheless, it was all experience. War, like death, had a habit of concentrating the mind. Better to be there than to be curing Mrs Jones' sniffles in some dingy one horse town in the middle of nowhere. He would learn the job on his feet. Or maybe even on his knees.

He also watched the politics of the Holy Land cause pain for many people. In France he saw the pain of exhaustion at the end of the war, and the joy of freedom. In Greece the same pain was compounded by poverty.

There are many stories he remembers from these years but perhaps the most intriguing was the story of a pilot with an unusual problem.

The sergeant in charge of the sick quarters told him one day that Flight-Lieutenant Sergei I. Komaroff had arrived. Malachy said to put him on a couch and he would see him. Sergei was a Russian. He'd found his way to England in some strange and mysterious manner. He was a night-fighter with his squadron. Three weeks previously he had been wounded in the side. The gunner was his own flight commander, the ultimate irony.

Malachy went in to see Sergei, who sat on a stool. He certainly looked Russian. His head was round with tufted black hair and a very black beard. His small eyes twinkled with a good-humoured smile. In stature he was broad-shouldered, stocky and a little below average height.

As Malachy examined his wound he said, 'Doctor, you need not be afraid of hurting me.' Malachy replied, 'I know.' Sergei wasn't only unusual in being an officer in the RAF, he was also unique in that he couldn't feel pain. He was born that way. He looked at Malachy with relish as he failed to cause even a semblance of pain with needle prick, scalpel, stab or searing electric cautery applied to his skin. It gave him much satisfaction to be painless.

But this blessing was in its own way a curse, a malady of another sort.

Because of his unusual absence of a normal warning sensory system, Sergei had to be very wary of his skin. He had to watch like a hawk lest it be cut or lacerated. Almost casually he demonstrated that he had no trouble feeling coins in his pocket and bringing them out. It wasn't sensation of any kind he lacked, just the particular sensation of pain.

If Sergei walked across cut glass in his bare feet he wouldn't feel anything. His only salvation would be his eyes. They would see the blood.

Perhaps the most famous person unable to feel pain was the 1920s vaudeville artist Edward Gibson, who often invited audiences to stick needles into him after his shows. Like Sergei he seemed to be delighted with this. He called himself 'The Human Pin Cushion'.

Not surprisingly, many of these people die young. They're forever damaging their organs without knowing it, causing both external and internal bruising. Even chest pain that warns of an imminent coronary is lost to them.

Sergei's opposite was a flight sergeant whose plane was hit by shrapnel. His crew appeared to be uninjured and landed safely. The pilot, however, was suffering from severe pain in the tips of his fingers. Examination showed no obvious injury. His X-rays were normal but he continued to complain bitterly of an intolerable burning pain. Re-examination showed a tiny puncture wound in his wrist which Malachy explored. The track led down to the large nerve in front of the wrist, the median nerve. Embedded in its sheath was a small piece of plastic material, a substance used in the windshields of aircraft. Malachy took it out and the pain was gone the following day. In this man's case pain was a better diagnostician than the X-rays. Was he luckier than Sergei? In some ways, yes.

Malachy filed away incidents like these in the back of his mind, becoming increasingly fascinated by the subject of pain. There seemed to be an infinite variety of ways in which people could be afflicted by it. It could be sharp or aching, burning or tingling, numbing or nauseating. In some instances it could even shoot to distant parts of the body than the obvious danger areas. It could also be dormant, the worst kind of all because it left a doctor nothing to work with. There was even phantom pain, which some soldiers felt in war-zones after their legs and/or arms had been amputated.

Another kind of pain was called causalgia. This was usually due to injury of a peripheral nerve in a limb. It meant the slightest movement brought on paroxyms of agony. Even the scraping of a chair on the floor or a high musical note could cause severe pain to this kind of sufferer. Usually these people didn't want anyone to come close to them as even the movement of air on the affected area was unbearable.

A condition similar to analgesia was what doctors called idiopathic pain. (They sometimes joked that it got this name because the doctor is an idiot and the patient pathetic!) It wasn't funny, however, when the pain was so chronic it drove people to depression and sometimes even suicidal thoughts. At the very least it caused them to become more withdrawn and anti-social. Often too it led to addiction to painkillers. Such painkillers usually had little effect beyond causing this very addiction.

Patients who failed to have their symptoms treated or properly diagnosed (understandably) lost faith in their doctors, or else it worked the other way round, i.e. the doctor had trouble believing *them*. This, of course, shouldn't happen because all pain is real to the patient whether it has a psychosomatic element or not. If it's primarily in his or her imagination, it's still 'there'.

In the old days unexplainable chronic pain was called 'psychogenic' but that term has now been done away with since doctors have come to realise all pain is in some way psychological. If a doctor is stumped as regards a cure he may try to reassure a patient by letting them know they have no serious illness. Alternatively, he may prescribe placebos. These will only work if the psychological element of the pain radically supersedes the physical one. If all else fails patients may have to accept the pain, whatever its cause, as a constant in their lives. This acceptance usually opens the door to a better quality of life in that it enables them to keep it at bay to some degree. Pain management clinics can also help.

An anaesthesiologist called Henry Beecher conducted an important study on placebos during World War II. He interviewed a number of soldiers who had been wounded on the Italian front and were being treated in hospital. He was astounded that many of those who were seriously wounded were markedly uninterested in receiving painkillers. Indeed, when asked about their pain, they trivialised it. In contrast, many of them winced when they received basic injections.

He concluded from this strange set of circumstances that they weren't immune to pain as such, but their relief at being away from the fray was so intense that they had actually 'blocked' the pain from their combat injuries. Some of them were even elated. A hospital injection, on the contrary, didn't belong to this context of pain management, which is why it elicited the extreme reaction from them. For Beecher this proved just how huge a part the brain – or, more specifically, the thalamus – played in assessing degrees of pain.

There's a scene in the film *All the President's Men* where a man places his hand over the flame of a candle and leaves it there even as it burns him. Hs face shows no reaction to the burning flesh. 'What's the trick?' his friend enquires. 'The trick is not minding,' he replies, somewhat facetiously. Beecher made a similar type of point.

Referred or phantom pain isn't only the preserve of amputees; it can assail any of us. A pain in the left arm, for instance, is a sign that there's a problem with the heart. A shooting pain down the leg suggests a back problem. So does a certain type of foot pain. Cancer may also first exhibit itself in 'secondary' pain, far from where the main problem lies. However it's in amputees that we see the syndrome most clearly. We should also include those who have mastectomies and hysterectomies in this category. The former frequently experience sensations in the breast area and the latter in the womb, often in the form of enigmatic menstrual cramps.

When a limb is amputated, the brain takes time to adjust. It isn't geared to deal with such an absence so it becomes confused. A sort of 'time lapse' situation takes root. We might make an analogy to a phone line that keeps ringing even though the account has been terminated, or even perhaps to the aftershock of an earthquake. Put prosaically, there's a delayed reaction.

Those who have had a hand or foot amputated may be extremely sensitive to the wind, or a light piece of clothing touching the area of amputation, where a cluster of severed nerve ends may be in a state of chaos. These nerve ends send messages to the brain to be concerned about this particular area. They tell it to worry, in effect, or to make the hand or leg throb. It might be a tickle or a burning sensation. Some patients experience sudden tingles almost akin to electric shocks.

Malachy once came across a religious sect that actually welcomed pain. They offered it up for their sins and the sins of others, like ancient monks who practised masochistic rituals for similar purgative purposes. Such individuals, he noted, were very economical from a drug point of view!

Non-religious masochists also inflict pain on themselves, either for some perverse thrill or as a kind of sublimated guilt. The poets C.S. Lewis once referred to pain as 'God's megaphone'. Similarly, many people – bringing us into the religious field again – welcome it as a form of expiation.

Mother Teresa used to speak of the 'privilege' of pain.

9

Towards the end of the war Malachy became Medical Officer to a corps of troops that had been captured from the army of Field Marshal Erwin Rommel, the so-called 'desert fox'.

After the defeat of the Italian Army in Libya at the end of 1940, Hitler knew that if he wanted to keep Italy in the war, and, by extension, his Southern Mediterranean flank free from interference, a blocking force of troops was needed in North Africa to halt his army's retreat and bolster their morale. He chose Rommel, a decorated infantryman from World War I who had ascended from the rank of Lieutenant Colonel to Field Marshal within a mere four years, to lead this new force. (He had also had substantial success in this war with his Afrika Corps). It officially came into being on February 19, 1941.

Rommel conducted his desert campaign across North Africa for the next two years, first against Britain and then the U.S. He was an intense, ruthless general. Rumour has it he gunned down a French POW one day simply because he refused to get into a vehicle Rommel had ordered him into. A passionate and driven man, he conducted his desert campaign with great guile. His trademark riding boots and airman's goggles resting on his peaked cap were as recognisable as the swastika itself. He was the bright jewel in the arid desert, a man who showed great devotion to his wife – like Malachy's she was also called Lucy – and also his soldiers. He was particularly drawn to the younger ones, infecting them with his own passion for victory.

Nobody underestimated Rommel's military genius. Winston Churchill, no less, was once heard to exclaim, 'What else matters but beating him?' He famously said himself, 'The battle is fought and decided by the quartermasters before the shooting begins'. And so it proved. But Rommel had a mercurial temperament, and when things went against him he lost his judgment. In attack he was exemplary, in retreat vulnerable.

He chased the Eighth Army back toward the Nile in the summer of 1942 but he suffered a heavy defeat at the battle of El Alamein and had been retreating since. His health was also in a poor state by now. Beset with rheumatism, exhaustion, low blood pressure and intestinal problems, his leadership qualities were deteriorating. His army had been bolstered by reinforcements from Italy – the remnants of Mussolini's imperial force in Libya but he had little respect for these, imagining they were poorly trained and badly equipped. The standard Italian rifle dated back to 1891, and some of the soldiers were well nigh-illiterate, so much so that drill instructors had to tie bandannas round their left arms to teach them left from right. Many of them fought vigorously, but others, as one official put it, were more interested in 'coffee, cigarettes and women' than the war. Rightly or wrongly, Rommel blamed them for his problems.

Rommel's end was heralded in unlikely fashion by Britain's General Bernard Montgomery, who was delegated at short notice to do battle with him. He knew it wasn't going to be easy. Monty held Rommel in awe, as did his own troops. He knew he led by example, that he wasn't so much a dictator as one who let it be known he would go down with his men.

Like Rommel, Montgomery was a hero of World War I. Both were exemplary strategists. When they engaged in combat it wasn't so much cat-and-mouse as fox versus hound – Teutonic efficiency versus British doggedness. Montgomery relished the challenge of taking on a man whose reputation was legendary. If he could unseat him he knew he could become a legend himself. And so it came to pass. By defeating his renowned adversary, he saved Egypt, Malta and the Middle East from the clutches of the Nazis. The battle of El Alamein was, in a sense, the beginning of the end for Hitler. For Montgomery it was proof of his durability on the world's stage. Cometh the man, cometh the moment.

Rommel was a broken man after El Alamein. He ordered his troops to pull back, despite an edict from Hitler himself to fight to the bitter end. On December 3, 1942 his army was in full retreat, leaving behind 50 destroyed panzers, another 50 abandoned anti-tank guns and over 400 other vehicles. Hitler was rumoured to have bitten the carpet in rage when he heard the news. His beloved Field Marshal had finally fallen from grace.

The following month he was implicated in a putsch to overthrow Hitler by being named as its spearhead by a band of conspirators who were alleged to have given his name under torture. Hitler thereby issued his erstwhile military darling with an ultimatum: either take a quick-acting poison in front of his generals or submit to the ignominy of a tribunal. If he chose the former he was assured he would be given a state funeral and his wife a pension. This was enough to 'persuade' the man who had fought so relentlessly for so long to fall on his sword.

Hitler refused to allow Rommel to shoot himself – the death he would have preferred – being well aware of his great standing with the German people. He didn't want the scandal of a suicide. Poison allowed the Fuhrer to create the fiction that Rommel had died of a brain haemorrhage which he claimed had resulted from an accident he'd had shortly before when his car skidded on the road. (This had actually happened.) 'One of our best army leaders has passed away,' he said in his eulogy of him, disassociating himself from his death as he had from the deaths of so many others, both within his own ranks and those of the enemy.

Some soldiers deserted at this time and faced court martials as a result. This didn't deter them. They would even have preferred penal servitude to frontline action. One statistician put the number of deserters as high as 25,000 as Rommel's army surged onwards through the desert. To try and counteract this trend a General called Auchinleck repeatedly asked the War Office in London to bring back the death penalty.

This was rejected for two reasons. Firstly, it was established that the number of desertions in World War I was actually greater than the present one. Considering the death penalty was 'in' during the earlier war, such a realisation effectively knocked the deterrent factor of the ultimate punishment on the head. Secondly, even if the Eighth Army approved of executing deserters, people at home in Britain might not. The reintroduction of the death penalty would also highlight the desperate nature of the desertion problem and create a feeling that the army was losing its way, or failing to show proper authority in the face of distress.

Leaving things as they were proved the wiser course of action because it wasn't long before Rommel's Afrika Corps went into retreat. The deserters then returned to their units and suffered little more than the ignominy of being stripped of their rank. Some of them re-enlisted in elite units like the SAS and the Long Range Desert Group on the understanding that they could 're-earn' their stripes if they fought arduously for the rest of the war. This many were inclined to do, morale being higher now that Rommel was on the run. Those who failed to show any such initiative, or remorse, were either denied early demobilisation or given menial tasks to perform. Some of them, as was the case in Exeter, were suffering from genuine shellshock rather than a failure of nerve. One soldier was alleged to have tried to 'dig a hole' through his bed in an attempt to evade the enemy. He imagined he was in a bunker and wanted to make it deeper. Others ran round hospital wards in a frenzy at the merest hint of gunfire, imagining they were in the thick of the action again.

'In the early days', as the author Ben Shephard put it, 'the desert war had an addictive, romantic quality to it. It was a return in a machine age to the knightly duelling of the past. it was war purged of inessentials like civilians, an expression of masculine courage and sporting endeavour.' As time went on, however, lengthy confinement in tanks and loss of sleep, combined with the knowledge that the Germans were better armed, led to pressures even greater than those experienced in the trenches. One may have had greater power at one's disposal than a private in a foxhole, but one was also an open target to be taken down on sight. Watching one's friends burn to death in this manner was an experience hardly to be relished. Even worse was the decision sometimes forced upon a tank commander to abandon his own crew to what Shepherd calls 'their fiery fate' inside a doomed tank. Riding in the turret he could get out at the sight of danger, but they couldn't. That left a nasty aftertaste. And, for some, terrible incapacitating depression.

Many soldiers went to Cairo to unwind. Malachy sometimes joined them, on one occasion cavorting with a bellydancer on the stage of the opera house where Verdi's *Aida* was first performed (He's reluctant to go into any detail about this experience save to say that his dancing partner of the evening seemed to have curves in places other women didn't even have places.)

The location of the camp where these prisoners were interred was in the south east of the Sahara desert. It had an officer's mess with fifteen soldiers and a C.O. There were about 3,000 POWs and they came from all walks of life: chefs, bankers, plumbers, tailors, teachers, a chemist and even an opera singer.

In the film *The Bridge on the River Kwai*, Alec Guinness put his men to work on building the eponymous bridge. For a time it became therapy, but eventually Guinness became obsessed with it. Teetering on the borders of insanity, he all but forgot what country he was fighting for, his soldiers aiding and abetting 'the enemy'.

Malachy would hardly go to such lengths. His demands were more modest than a bridge. He simply set about finding out what professions the prisoners had and letting them exercise them.

One military strategist described prisoners of war as being similar to deep sea divers returning to the surface of the water. As such, they needed the psychological equivalent of the kind of decompression chamber Malachy elected to enter some time before. He knew it was in his own interests from a practical point of view to keep the POWs content. If nothing else, it meant they would be less likely to try and escape if they were gainfully occupied. Listlessness often led to groundless fears and half-baked attempts to get back to their own units. Such attempts would have very long odds of success but desperation drove men to low percentage gambits.

He and his colleagues were interested in finding anyone that could be useful to them, a search that met with some success when they discovered a bespoke tailor. Malachy immediately set him to work making a coat for him. He also found a watchmaker. Thereafter all watches in the camp started working smoothly.

The prisoners relished doing chores to pass the time. Malachy describes this phase of his life as 'a man-made heaven: heaven for us and an ameliorated hell for the POWs.'

They knew little about games. They'd never even heard of golf. Lucky things, he thought: it probably meant they suffered less stress. He eventually taught them to play soccer on a makeshift sandy pitch, their murky figures moving like elongated shadows against the westering sun. After the games they would come back to camp in high spirits, marching in long snake-like lines as they sang 'Lili Marlene' with mock-plaintiveness.

As time went on he started to build up a relationship with them, to get to grips with them as people. In a sense the war became almost an irrelevance. What did nationality matter? No more than the British, or himself, they were all caught like rabbits in the headlights of an oncoming car and trying to make the best of it. He didn't want neurotics on his hands, or men paralysed with fear. He remembered the German pilot who thought he was going to be tortured. Maybe these men had been filled with the same propaganda. It was time to get rid of the jingoistic fears that had been whipped up.

Each morning he ran a regular sick parade, treating his patients for such various maladies as snake bites, diarrhoea, headaches and fevers. One day the sergeant remarked to him that since Germans reputedly liked order, he should put labels of ailments above the entrances to the sick bay for convenience.

This he did. Over one entrance was the message: 'If you have a headache, enter here'. The patient in question went in to through the entrance, collected his aspirin and left through a door marked 'Exit', without having seen anyone. It worked like clockwork, even for the diarrhoea patients. (No doubt the Irish health service could take some pointers from this exemplary efficiency.)

He spent a lot of his time learning German in his tent, thereafter trying out his new-found skills on the prisoners. At one point he learned a German drinking song, 'Trinken Wiv Nocht Ein Fropcken Aus Dem Kleine Henkelpotchen', which means 'Once more we will moisten our lips from the dear little cup with a grip'. One day during a kitchen inspection with the sergeant he saw two young blonde chefs and asked them if they could sing the song. They immediately sprang to attention and started trying to sing it under his instruction. They took it as an order to be complied with for fear of redress!

The nights were generally quiet. A bright moon shone and the sky was dotted with brilliant stars. One night as he was sleeping in his tent he was awakened by a faint rustling. He had a sense that something was moving outside. When he switched on his light he saw a black hand edging towards the small clock that stood on his bedside locker. A moment later, after jumping up and opening his tent flap, he saw a fleeing figure silhouetted against the sky. A shot rang out then and the figure swerved before disappearing between the other tents. It transpired that one of Malachy's fellow officers had fired at him but missed.

He went back to bed, but the next day examined the footprints in the sand. Amazingly, his clock was in one of the indentations. The thief had obviously dropped it when the shot flew past him.

It appeared uncanny to Malachy that anything could exist in the barren terrain of the desert. There were many antelopes which were hunted for their meat. Scorpions also abounded and loved getting into the sandbags round the tents. One night he was called out to see what was wrong with a soldier who was lying on the sand, unable to move. There was no sign of injury but an examination of the sole of his foot showed a small fracture there, with blood oozing from it. He'd been stung by a scorpion, having disobeyed orders by walking around in his bare feet. He suffered temporary paralysis as a result.

Another thing that intrigued Malachy was the fine sand that ran through the dunes like little rivulets. You could run into these hollows and feel as if you were in the middle of a deep stream. They were called 'wadis'.

He once saw a wedding in progress. The bride was dressed in white and wore a veil and head-dress. She sat apart from the rest of the wedding party on a camel's hump as the animal trundled along, kicking little clouds of sand about with his large flat feet, the lady's veil appearing and disappearing as he passed each sand dune. The sergeant turned to Malachy and said, 'That's probably a Christian marriage.' Malachy agreed that the camel definitely looked like a Catholic.

A group wearing gallabiyas followed her. These are long white dresses worn by the Fellaheen which drop like sacks from the shoulders to the feet. They swing in the wind and blow the mosquitoes and flies away as they do so.

Malachy's camp was situated 1000 miles south of the Mediterranean almost in a direct line from El Alamein, the site of the battle where most of his prisoners were captured. One day he was driving in his four-wheeled jeep with his commanding officer when he spotted a group of Arab surveyors along with some civilians and camels. They were beside a mine-field and treading gingerly around it. He was dumbstruck when he saw three women crossing the minefield without a care in the world as they proceeded to the cleared zone.

At this time he was living in the sick quarter, a rather basic edifice built of cement blocks. Here he had a batman who tended to his every need. His name was Said-Ahmed, plus a number of other appellations. He was so primitive he didn't even recognise his own face in a photograph. He did, however, make excellent tea. All Malachy had to say was 'Shai' and the required brew would be hastily served up. He was exceedingly deferential, but totally ignored everyone when he was on his prayer mat. He prayed six times a day, lying prostrate on the ground as he did so.

One day an Arabian woman from a nearby village called Kafareet presented herself at the sick quarter without an appointment. She was very badly burned. Strictly speaking he wasn't supposed to treat anybody outside his immediate remit but she was in such a bad way he gave her morphine and some antibiotics to bring down the inflammation. He asked the sergeant of the division to keep this confidential. When she was leaving he saw scores of villagers sitting on their hunkers outside. They had all come to watch. They were deeply indebted to him for treating her. She had burned herself with cooking oil and they realised how ill she was. As a token of appreciation they made a beautiful silk scarf for Malachy. Its cost, he believes, would have been equivalent to the total income of the entire village for a whole year. He was sincerely touched by the gesture and kept the scarf as a memento.

He eventually got an office in Cairo, and also treated patients in Port Said on the Suez Canal. Ships came in with sick servicemen on board and he tended these. Often he organised air transport home for them.

In his spare time he played RAF league rugby, his 'career' being cut short by some ugly tackles from an Australian team. He's not a great fan of Australian rules (or should it be called Australian lack of rules?) as a result.

He also took up golf at this time. Injuries were less prevalent here. In fact all that got hurt, he says, was his pride.

One day he went to a soccer match in a large stadium in Cairo. Just as he settled himself in his seat the other spectators started clambering over the barriers and pouring out onto the pitch. He thought a riot had started and held his breath but all that was happening was that it was half-time (he had arrived late) and they were going to pray. Their kneeling figures completely covered the pitch, all facing the one way: towards Mecca. He was mightily relieved.

As a medical officer in the RAF, Malachy had to attend important meetings bearing on operational matters. As a result he was aware of all plans for raids and missions that were imminent. Such information proved valuable to him on one particular occasion: when he met Pope Pius XII in Rome. It was at a time of the war when Italy had collapsed and the Germans were scattered throughout the country in undisclosed locations. (His tour of duty in the Middle East had ended by now and he was posted to Italy.)

Rome was still under threat of bombardment and the Pope was particularly concerned about the danger. In the days leading up to Italy's surrender, the government that deposed Mussolini had declared Rome an 'Open City', i.e. a demilitarised zone. The Pope prayed that this declaration would preserve its wonders from devastation. Was it too much to ask that the Coliseum be preserved? He quoted the ancient prophecy: 'When falls the Coliseum, Rome shall fall/And when Rome falls – the world!' Hitler was now a wounded animal and everyone knew how dangerous that species could be, having nothing to lose now. Mussolini had also nothing to lose. 'Whosoever raises his hand against Rome,' the Pope declared, 'will be guilty of manslaughter before the civilised world, and the eternal judgment of God.' But inside himself he was terrified of the fate of the Eternal City.

Rome may not have been built in a day, but it could have been destroyed in one. All the architectural genius of aeons could have been wiped out overnight on the whim of a deposed demagogue who wanted to bring something down with him. It was too horrific to contemplate.

Malachy felt he could allay the Pope's fears, having been informed through his network of sources that it was unlikely any great damage would be done there.

On his way to Rome he saw battered tanks and burned-out vehicles. When he got there he headed for Vatican City with a fellow officer, nursing an ambition to have an audience with the Pope. This was finally achieved through a friend. Himself and a small group of servicemen were ushered into the Papal chambers and soon afterwards Pope Pius arrived, acknowledging each officer as he moved between them. He greeted Malachy in English, looking intently at him as he examined his uniform.

Without thinking, Malachy suddenly reached forward and touched the cuff of the pontiff's sleeve. 'Rome will not be harmed,' he blurted out, almost unconsciously. The Pope blessed him in response. He felt a mixture of elation and guilt inside himself. He hadn't been given any authority to impart this information but nonetheless felt he'd done the right thing, regardless of protocol. But he wouldn't have done it for anyone else. How could you not tell the Pope his city was safe?

At 1.41 on Monday, 7 May 1945, the war ended. A week previously Hitler had poisoned Eva Braun, his wife of a day and a half, and then shot himself in the temple in his bunker. His dream of world conquest, like Germany itself, was reduced to rubble. But the world would never be the same again. It was as if a beast had unleashed itself not only in Adolf Hitler but in everyone who fought with him and for him – and even against him. Peace had arrived, but at a price. Now everybody knew how low they could sink to stay alive.

Seven months later as night was falling on Castleblaney, a lorry passed up Main Street carrying oranges, the first consignment to appear in the town for six years. It was a potent symbol of life returning to normal and people gaped at it on the street the way a besieged city might have gaped at the sudden influx of Allies. Hitler was dead and the guns were silent. From now on, Malachy surmised, he would have few patients with shrapnel wounds. He could get on with the business of trying to find cures for persistent maladies instead of putting his finger in the dam of wanton destruction.

10

As a result of his war service, Malachy was given a grant to cover two years of training. This would prepare him to become a fellow of one of the Royal Colleges of Surgeons. There were three of these but he chose the one in Edinburgh.

He did so because of its hallowed tradition. It had been founded in 1505 from the Corporation of Barber-Surgeons, receiving its charter from James IV the following year. Since then many world-famous professors passed through its doors: Robert Sibbald, Archibald Pitcairne, James Halket, John Hope, Archibald Menzies, John McLaren, James Lind, Andrew Duncan, James Syme, James Young Simpson, Henry Littlejohn, Joseph Lister, Sir Robert Philip, even Sir Arthur Conan Doyle. Would he one day be able to emulate any of their achievements? It was a daunting challenge.

The main building was Graeco-Roman. Inside was a repository of surgical history. Adjacent to this was the Royal Infirmary, a famous teaching hospital. He could live near both, an ideal setting to inspire him.

As part of the grant he was given a temporary job in the infirmary. This gave him access to the wards, the clinics and the operating theatres. It was a valuable adjunct to academic study.

The lectures were erudite and sophisticated. You weren't just trained to be a surgeon, you were taught the principles *behind* surgery. Once these were mastered and understood, the rest followed. The 'carpentry' component of surgery wasn't stressed. A man could perform many operations and still not know his stuff. There were nuances that had to be learned if you wanted to become more than what one of his professors called 'a glorified plumber'.

There were fifty doctors doing the same course for the Fellowship. They were from various parts of the world including Australia, New Zealand, South Africa and India. They all hoped to become Fellows, but only about 20% of them passed the exams on average. Some tried a second time but others gave up the ghost without achieving their greatest ambition. They wouldn't have F.R.C.S. after their names so would 'just' be called Doctor.

The general public understood the meaning of the prestigious letters. They were assured they would receive the highest standard of surgical care. The stamp was there and was trusted without question. They didn't need to shop around to find out who was a reputable surgeon and who wasn't. The weeding-out process had begun at age fourteen. Only the most capable survived.

In a sense, he surmised, it was similar to the professional golfer. Only the scratch handicap players got into the big tournaments. After passing the Fellowship examination, four years followed where a form of apprenticeship had to be performed. Here the budding surgeon had to master the art and the craft. He worked with one surgeon, couldn't practice on his own and received a small salary. Only after this was he eligible to have a private practice of his own or work as a full-time consultant on salary in a hospital or clinic.

Despite this arduous regimen, some still didn't become capable surgeons. There were many X factors involved, like instinctive judgement, a feeling for tissues, a flair for the job, a certain boldness. All of these qualities were needed to make up the complete package. Some students, for one reason or another, couldn't deal with the stress of the job, which was fairly ubiquitous. Some had no vocation, others were poor general managers. A few of them were attracted to the speciality in theory but had no stomach for the blood and guts. These men often found a slot in academia, becoming hurlers on the surgical ditch.

Malachy's priorities were more basic. He felt he had little time to waste. Almost five years had been carved out of his life by the war and he was anxious to make them up.

Doctors, like soldiers, also had teething pains when it came to re-adjusting to civilian life. In his case the problem would be compounded by the fact that he hadn't been a player in the game of war but rather someone on the periphery taking notes. You won no medals for bravery when you wiped the blood from a wounded man's face, or even when you amputated his legs. Removing the wedding ring from a dead man's hand made one feel more like an embalmer than a surgeon. No wonder so many war correspondents ended up with nerve problems even greater than those they wrote about. He would be hard put to forget some of the nightmarish things he'd seen.

His only saving grace was that he'd been too busy to take a lot of it in when it was happening. Like the twisted spools of a horror movie he would try to come to grips with it, unscrambling it if and when the time came to, quote unquote, rehabilitate himself. Until then he would just go with the flow – if there was one.

Maybe now that he was back in the world where his sleep wasn't disrupted by bullets and sirens, the possibility of work would stop too. After being thrown in at the deep end he mightn't find a secure spot in the shallow one. Life had a habit of being either this feast or famine.

Mornings were spent at the hospital, afternoons in the medical library and in the College's museum. The evenings were devoted to study in his rooms. He had a huge amount of knowledge and information to amass. It seemed impossible to him that he could read all the books he was supposed to.

He had, however, learned the knack of quickly skimming through a chapter in a book. He always searched for the key piece of information, the core of the matter. He memorised this and this alone. He also jotted it down. It was all he needed to know. Later on he would hang pieces of information onto this core. He applied the same method to lectures, distilling and keeping the distillate in his mind. He could usually recall it. This in turn would give him more. Many of the doctors tried feverishly to take down all a lecturer said. They collected voluminous notes that they couldn't read again. In many cases, the detail hid the central theme.

Near Malachy's classrooms and the hospital was the Museum. Founded long before the discovery of anaesthetics, it literally teemed with history and tradition. In those days not too much surgery could be performed because the pain was unbearable. In an age before morphine and the like mitigated this, many people were simply left to die.

One operation that *was* performed was limb amputation. This was, of course, extremely shocking and brutal. Speed and dexterity were the prerequisites. The surgeons needed only these qualifications for success. They could amputate an arm or a leg in a few minutes. The operation was successful, but the patient often died! (It was, however, better than lying in agony on a battlefield after being transfixed by a sword and trampled on by charging cavalry).

In the museum, among thousands of other pathological specimens, were a series of about ten human skulls. They were arranged on a shelf facing outward. Each skull had a long fissure fracture about six inches long running obliquely across the dome. They all seemed to be parallel. They were the skulls of soldiers killed by Turkish cavalrymen in a battle near the pyramids in the 19th century. He could visualise the galloping horses with riders astride them, rhythmically striking the heads of infantrymen with oriental scimitars. As he looked at the skulls he saw the precision of the sword-strokes. This might have taken the glamour out of war for him, but such glamour had already been well and truly guillotined in the years between 1939 and 1945. It was one thing to read about military combat in a book, another to see it up close and personal.

War simplified life – and death. There were no compromises, no grey areas. The side that inflicted the most damage on the opposing army was likely to win. Those with severe pain weren't going to fight anymore. Their will to resume combat the next day would surely have been gone. Neither were there any prizes for coming second.

The British TV war cameraman Nick Downie once said, 'The best way to convince man that war is not an exciting adventure is to kill half his friends, drop a bomb on his family's house, and relieve him of a limb or two. A less drastic but quite effective form of education is to show events like these on colour television.' Maybe such words were relevant when Downie spoke them, in 1980, but today we even seem immune to slaughter on television if the Gulf War and, latterly, the war in Iraq, are yardsticks. Perhaps suicide bombers in Israel are also accepted as an inalienable facet of life, their fates sandwiched between the weather report and the sports bulletins on Sky News.

It seemed disingenuous, somehow, to try and philosophise while shells were going off all around you. Ideologies created conflict, but it wasn't the ideologies that died: it was the common soldier riding high on a wing and a prayer, somebody like Max Redford who thought of it all like a boyish adventure until he stopped a bullet.

As if to add insult to injury, it wasn't people like Max who captivated the public, but rather celebrities who had done much less in life.

When Malachy was at the Royal Infirmary, King George IV was stricken with severe pain in one of his legs when he walked. The cause of the pain was found to be due to a diminution of the blood supply to the leg, particularly the muscles of the calf. The underlying pathology was damage to the wall of the main artery to the leg and to muscle spasm in this vessel.

A Scottish professor called Learmonth lectured Malachy on vascular disease. He'd done much research on these conditions in the laboratory associated with the hospital. He achieved worldwide fame as an erudite authority on arterial dysfunction and disease. The spotlight fell on him and he was controversially chosen as the surgeon to treat the king. It was an accolade. A sense of pride pervaded the infirmary. Edinburgh felt honoured.

After assessing the clinical findings and analysing laboratory data it was decided that a surgical form of treatment offered the best chance of improving the effects of the condition.

The operation decided upon was to relieve the spasm in the arteries by dividing some nerves deep in the lower back. These nerves lying close to the spine controlled the calibre of the arteries.

Learmonth's complete vascular and surgical unit moved to Buckingham Palace. Here, in a regal enclave, they set up their own temporary operating-room. In due course the surgery was carried out. It was successful and there were no complications. It was like being in a fishbowl with the world looking on. When the professor returned, Malachy saw no change in his demeanour. He remained a humble and straightforward Scotsman.

The king died some years later from lung cancer. He had been a heavy smoker all his life. This had damaged his arteries and then his lungs.

Apart from some improvement in the main limb arteries, the surgery on him improved the nutrition of his skin. This helped to prevent the occurrence of ulcers, a complication of the condition. Once an ulcer was formed, infection ensued. The whole litany of misery was compounded. This cycle usually ended in amputation, sometimes of both lower limbs. The pain was of enormous magnitude, and all self-inflicted by the smoking.

Have we learned anything at all since the time of King George? Maybe Mary Harney could answer that one for us.

11

Another event now happened in Malachy's life that was to change it dramatically: he fell in love. During a holiday at a doctor friend's house in Ireland he went to a party and there met Lucy O'Hara, a Sligo girl who was helping her father in his plumbing business. She was also breeding dogs for show purposes and won a couple of prizes at the Dublin Dog Show in Ballsbridge. As well as this she was a gifted golfer, having been given many lessons in Rosses Point by none other than Christy O'Connor, who would go on to become Ireland's most famous exponent of the sport.

When Malachy started dating her she was able to beat him quite easily, which resulted in her giving him a stroke for each hole they played. Golf, of course, was very much a secondary consideration for the woosome twosome at this time.

It was love at first sight and they were hardly out of each other's reach for the next six months. When he finally proposed to her she said she had something very important to tell him before she could answer him. 'I can't have children,' she confessed. The news came as a surprise to him but it didn't affect his feelings for her one whit. 'That doesn't matter to me if we have each other,' he said, and her eyes welled up with tears.

They got married in the Cathedral of the Immaculate Conception in Sligo on September 30th, 1952. One chapter in his life had ended and another was about to begin.

Not long afterwards they found themselves occupying a small suite in the Grand Hotel in Paris, Malachy having been awarded a Travelling Fellowship in Europe that allowed him to review orthopaedic practice in other cities. He chose Rome, Paris and Bologna. They went to Paris first, as a kind of unofficial honeymoon.

It seemed to epitomise all the possibilities of his future. Where better could he be at this time of his life? He had his love and his career. It was like he'd reached a crossroads in this historic city. With Lucy he explored its art and architecture, the whole place oozing with vibrancy. It was the chic capital of Europe and also had innovative medical experiments going on. He wanted, needed, to be a part of all that. He had so much enthusiasm, no negative experience could blunt it. He felt like a *tabula rasa* upon which life would write its instructions.

Their first few days had no pattern but that was as it should have been. What honeymoon worth its salt had a plan? They let time take them where it would, the days blending into one another as they soaked up the chaos. He felt he was escaping into some forbidden place, somewhere light years away from everything he'd known until now. They were drunk on the excitement of it, too adrenalised to sleep.

They spent much time in the Louvre. They also visited the Moulin Rouge and the Sacre Coeur – strange bedfellows – and walked all the way from the Arc de Triomphe to Rue de la Concorde.

The mornings were used for visiting tourist haunts, the afternoons for exercise and some work. At night it was like a different city as they strolled down the boulevards watching people driving manically, haranguing one another and honking their horns in sudden frustration. Others kissed and caressed in full view of them, unlike in Ireland where bashfulness held sway. In such an atmosphere they also became more spontaneous, ridding themselves of their native inhibitions.

They chatted to the people selling their wares on the street, some of whom looked like they were on the vague fringes of crime. They haggled good-humouredly with them before moving on. Elsewhere, neon-lit windows invited them into shows. Everything seemed exaggerated, as if a surprise lay round every corner. It seemed an ideal place to be. 'Pinch me to make sure it's real,' Lucy demanded. Any moment they thought they were going to wake up and find it was all a dream. Ernest Hemingway once described Paris as a moveable feast. They wondered if that feast could be moved back to where they would spend the rest of their lives or if it was going to end here in this frenetic bubble.

'Being broke in London is miserable,' the actress Kristin Scott Thomas said once, 'but being broke in Paris is quite nice.' There seemed to be something romantic in not having much money there. Students slept under the Eiffel Tower and in railway stations, getting their shoes kicked by the gendarmes in the mornings as they sought to clear the platforms for oncoming commuters. Afterwards he saw them down at the fruit markets eating the products that were going to be thrown away because of some deficiency. These youths, wrapped around each other's arms in puppy love, weren't too worried about quality control in such matters. They would live on fresh air.

One day when they were in the Louvre, Lucy was so exhausted from sight-seeing that she sat down on an antique chair. She was soon removed from it. The last person to have sat there, she was informed, was Louis

Quatorze. She was in good company.

Some evenings they sampled the exotic delights of La Pigale, the red-light district. On their second visit they ventured into a nightclub and were ushered to a small table in the dark. The madam of the establishment asked them what they'd like to drink. 'Come back in a while,' Malachy told her in pidgin French. She scowled.

At the end of the room under floodlights was a small stage where four women gyrated to the beat of primitive music. The doctor in Malachy noticed that they were sagging at vital points. It was obvious, he thought, that they needed a different kind of support than that of a dancing-pole. He also noticed that they were flatfooted, with little spring in their gait. Even as a voyeur he was still the surgeon extraordinaire!

Leering up at the dancers from other quarters of the nightclub were a group of bald old men, men who perhaps had left their wives at home to sample these busty phenomena struggling against gravity. Lucy O'Brien hardly needed to feel any such fears for her own husband. She might have reminded him of Mervyn Stockwood's definition of a psychiatrist: 'A man who goes to the Folies Bergeres and looks at the audience'.

After a while Madam appeared again to take their order, stamping her feet angrily when Malachy again told her he wasn't quite thirsty yet. At this point she informed him he had to either order a drink or leave. He chose the latter option. Outside, a tout tried to sell him pornographic pictures, indicating with a nod that if he ditched Lucy he had even more models to exhibit, perhaps even in the flesh.

He took a raincheck on this. If he'd entered a massage parlour, the chances were that he might have tried to cure some strumpet's sciatica rather than being the recipient of a massage himself.

12

The visit to the continent gave Malachy the chance to discuss orthopaedics with some of the most skilful practitioners in Europe and to learn what was right and wrong with the developing technology.

Professor Judet, a leading light in orthopaedic surgery, gave a cocktail party in honour of the visiting surgeons and aspiring novices. Malachy was amongst the latter. It was held in his chalet at St. Cloud, two miles west of Paris. It was on the left bank of the Seine and stood on a high ridge. From its large bow windows the river could be seen winding in gentle loops through tree-covered slopes. The chalet once belonged to Napoleon and himself and his mistress resided here. There was a steep gravel path from the main road up to it. Ominous-looking trees overhung its mossy verges. The famous painting of Napoleon on his white charger crossing the Alps gradually formed into a graphic image in Malachy's mind. He pictured him galloping through the pillared gateway and up the dark avenue after a hard day on the battlefield.

Professor Judet could have chosen a hotel in central Paris or at the University for his party. Instead he picked a venue with character and historical import. A cocktail party in the home of Napoleon's mistress! This was as good as it got.

Lucy and Malachy enjoyed themselves immensely mingling with the *distingué* of the orthopaedic world. The subject of Napoleon inevitably cropped up. A doctor told Malachy he travelled across Europe in a horse-drawn carriage. From a health viewpoint this was a wise choice for it saved the emperor much spinal compression and bone-jarring. It also saved his horse the same. But Napoleon actually used this mode of travel for a more businesslike purpose. He also spent a lot of time poring over maps spread out on the floor as he planned battle strategies. The latter activity hardly did his spine any favours, they concurred.

If there had been historians at the party, no doubt Napoleon's contribution to global events would have been the main talking-point, but Malachy was surrounded by people who seemed to think the conquest of nations came a poor second to vertebrae damage.

The question of how his back problems might have impacted on his love life wasn't explored, but if it was it might have given an added dimension to the famed, if apocryphal, phrase, 'Not tonight, Josephine!'

All the new doctors were in attendance. As befitted the local custom, they wore black hats on their heads. Each of them also had a gold ring placed on the left ring finger. It was symbolic of their 'marriage' to the university for the rest of their lives.

A large commitment, to be sure, but they had this kind of dedication. The war had just ended and pain was a huge issue. In one patient they discussed, a pain area was found in the centre of the brain. After this had been identified and then excised, referred pain in another part of the body was also relieved. This enigma would become Malachy's special area of concern in time.

The following day he travelled to a hospital to study the technique of a prestigious local surgeon. When he reached the operating-theatre, his assistants had already exposed the area to be dealt with and were awaiting the arrival of the surgeon. He finally entered, went straight to the operating table and performed the surgery in a few minutes. He then pulled off his gloves, gave everyone a quick nod and speedily departed the scene. Shortly afterwards they saw him in a heated discussion with somebody on a telephone.

In a corridor outside, a professor said to Malachy, 'He's a crusty old monument. He belongs to a past era. He's threatened by new orthopaedic developments and doesn't want to be confronted with them, preferring to put his head in the sand.' Malachy replied, 'Did you see his rubber gloves? They're the kind I use to wash my car.' He couldn't resist the sarcasm. Obviously the man had no respect for the generation coming after him. And, apparently, not much of a bedside manner with his patients. It was a bit like the pugnacious doctor who said to a patient one day, 'There are only two people who can help you in your condition: God and myself. And God is on holidays!' But sometimes the best doctors had the worst manner, and vice versa.

In his autobiography, *Dr John*, John O'Connell wrote about a consultant he served under who had a similarly stentorian personality. This man didn't refer to his patients by name, but rather as 'The Liver', 'The Heart' or 'The Kidneys'. In other words, they didn't exist as people but rather conditions. His name was Jack Henry and in O'Connell's view he should have been an Abbey actor. Henry's partypiece was an anecdote which concerned a man who couldn't urinate. One day Henry called to him to insert a catheter but before he could do anything the man dropped dead before his eyes. Henry always ended the story with this *piece de resistance*: 'The tragedy, gentlemen, was not that the patient died, but that my cheque lay unsigned on the mantelpiece.' (Perhaps he should have dispensed with the catheter and performed a 'cashectomy' instead.)

Another medical autobiography, John Fleetwood's *In Stitches*, also has an anecdote featuring an 'old school' consultant. Fleetwood is examining a pregnant woman in the out-patients department and he asks the students that are with him to make some comments on the patient. 'She's very advanced in her pregnancy,' one of them says. 'She has no stretch marks,' another ventures. A silence follows, which Fleetwood fills with the decidedly unPC comment, 'And she's got a fabulous pair of legs!' At this the curtain around the cubicle is pulled back and a consultant who has been listening to it all screams out, 'You do *not* tell a patient she has a fabulous pair of legs. This is a hospital, not a comedy store.' Fleetwood knew that the woman had been pleased with the comment, indeed flattered by it, and defended himself by saying that she didn't have a disease and therefore he felt the levity wouldn't do any harm. The consultant, who examined such patients not only without saying hello but even without looking at their faces, went off in high dudgeon. In his absence, Fleetwood took off his stethoscope and gave it to the woman, thereby allowing her to listen to the baby's heartbeat. This gratified her hugely.

Malachy also met a self-important surgeon in Bologna, a Professor Putti. He had his suits made in Saville Row and his laundry, according to reports, done in New York. A red carpet was rolled out for him as he arrived at the hospital. He stepped out of a swanky car. As he entered the hospital he looked like he owned it. Malachy was reminded of the old joke: What's the difference between God and an orthopaedic surgeon? Answer: God doesn't think he's an orthopaedic surgeon.

Rome was the next port of call for the newlyweds. They stayed at the Albergo Minerva in Piazza della Minerva, which wasn't quite as exotic as it sounded. Leaving Lucy to shop and sight-see, he visited a range of orthopaedic centres. Sadly, he wasn't very impressed with what was on view. The war had obviously taken its toll and everyone was busily picking up the pieces. Many of the doctors had actually been to England to catch up on the developments of the past six years, a curious reversal of the usual traffic.

Dining in the hotel proved too expensive so they sought out a local ristorante to satisfy their palates. The food was up to scratch but a recurring item on each night's bill caused them some concern. It was called 'Coperta', something they hadn't recalled ordering. Nonetheless, it was costing them many lira. They finally confronted the waiter about it, whereupon he reached for the edge of the tablecloth and raised it up.

'Coperta!' he beamed, grasping a fork and holding it aloft.

He then swivelled a chair around. 'Coperta!' he repeated. It slowly dawned on Malachy and Lucy that they weren't *eating* coperta, they were *using* it. It was a service charge.

They hadn't been used to this kind of thing in England. He objected to paying a toll to go through the door, lease the chair and rent the knives and forks.

He wondered if 'coperta' also included wear and tear on the floor, or the use of roof coverage. If he applied the same logic (or lack of it) to medicine, he felt sure he could have a lucrative sliding scale for pain relief. He could say to his patients, 'How much pain do you want taken away? See my chart outside for the rates.' In the case of wealthy patients, unscrupulous doctors could decide how sick to make them before relieving them of their money in incremental charges.

In the one hospital where he was designated to see an operation being performed, he wasn't allowed into the immediate operating area. Instead he had to watch the procedure through a glass dome directly over the operating table. This was useless to him. He knew he needed to be a mere centimetre away from the scalpel's edge. Four feet away might as well be forty feet. A fraction of a centimetre could, he knew, mean the difference between life and death. He needed to have a ringside seat. Otherwise he might as well have been watching the thing on television.

After Rome they moved on to Florence. Most of the people they met there were poor, which perhaps accounted for their irritable temperament. They weren't too concerned with medical developments, just in getting from day to day. He spent two days at a clinic. Orthopaedics, he found, was just a fledgling science in Florence, the surgeons young and inexperienced.

Most of them worked under adverse conditions. About four were operating at one time in a long narrow theatre. Each had a small stall of his own but little space. Bodies on trolleys kept moving in and out. Treated cases met new arrivals in the narrow passageway at the side of the operating-room. Patients going out were fully anaesthetised. Those coming in were wide awake and staring with anxiety at the sleeping, almost wraith-like figures passing them.

Outside in a large atrium was a scene of mass confusion. There was a rush of black-clothed women towards both sets of trolleys. Wives hung on to their husbands until the last minute as they were wheeled towards the door of the theatre. They were screaming and crying, but the attendant pulled them away. Another set of women descended on the emerging trolleys expecting to find their loved ones dead or maimed. They too had to be restrained as they were interfering with post-anaesthetic resuscitation.

Many of the doctors he spoke to were disgruntled and dissatisfied. Afterwards he explored the beauty of the old city with its great works of art and its ornate architecture, but somehow all of the historical monuments meant little. If anything, they only rubbed salt into the wounds of the all-too-recent war. An intangible fear hung in the air like a human thing, infecting everyone that breathed it. It was as if the dreaded Hun was still lying in wait to pounce on his victims.

Old memories died hard.

13

Malachy now moved into a large General Hospital in Hull in the northeast of England as a Senior Resident. It was the last few laps of his training. He was in an environment to properly assess what he'd learned in the past three and a half years.

His overall impression was of the cloying, omnipresent nightmare of pain everywhere he went. He felt it was being viewed in the wrong light. It was usually regarded as an entity in itself, as a sickness to be cured. He saw it more as a form of communication to be welcomed, a means rather than an end.

Pain, however, wasn't always a reliable friend. It could mislead as to the whereabouts of a given disease. Sometimes it indicated the wrong location in a mischievous manner. Circumstances also changed or mitigated it. There were situations in which movement caused pain and others where pain was caused by *lack* of movement. Sometimes cold caused pain and sometimes heat. There were no absolutes.

At Hull he distilled and then refined what he'd learned and observed. He was left with the conclusion that he knew very little really – a valuable starting-point.

All he could say for sure was that there were a huge number of conditions in the body, most of which produced this thing called pain. These conditions varied a lot on the surface but he wondered whether there was a common factor behind them all which might be the real clue. His mind considered some as yet unknown chemical neurological factor, either in the brain or the cord. He thought: If sorrow can cause tears, maybe pain is caused by some kind of internal weeping. In concepts like this, which have been taken up by so many psychosomatic theorists (if not homeopathic healers) in the generation to come, he was before his time.

In his wanderings, be it field hospital or great clinic, he'd come across cases where he was told, 'They haven't been able to find the cause of this man's problem', or 'They don't know the cause of the temperature in this woman.' Or 'This man's limp hasn't as yet been tracked down as to source.' In his latest assignment he came across cases that were truly baffling. Many patients were labelled 'NYD', which stood for 'Not yet diagnosed'.

Today, thankfully, this term isn't as prevalent as it was then. It hasn't quite become an endangered species yet, but in Malachy's time it was deployed almost as shorthand for every enigma. This wasn't so much due to laziness as ignorance.

After completing his general training he decided to specialise in orthopaedic surgery. He was fortunate to become assistant to the Senior Orthopaedic Surgeon at the hospital. Orthopaedics was a new specialty and was making great strides. Joint replacement surgery was becoming increasingly more successful. His experiences on the Continent had whetted his appetite for further investigations. He needed to be at the cutting edge of things – literally.

In the hospital where he worked there were two orthopaedic wards, one male and the other female. Each had 36 patients. All were confined to bed. Most were elderly and had broken their hips. Any attempt to bear weight on their damaged joints caused severe pain. They all had to abandon any hope, being relegated to the chronic wards. This meant that despite all efforts to help, nothing more of a medical or surgical nature could be done. They would never walk again.

Their plight was actually worse than that. Even in bed they suffered. They couldn't turn or move without discomfort. At night they would wake up with a sudden pain in the hip from moving involuntarily during a fitful sleep.

Their hips had fractured because they were elderly and their bones had become soft and brittle. Eventually they couldn't bear the weight of their own bodies and the hip gave way under the stress. The globular head of the thigh bone died.

Strenuous efforts were made to fix these fractures surgically using various forms of nails and plates. These were initially made of steel or vitallium. While such rudimentary stratagems weren't successful, a lot was learned. It was found, for instance, that after a plate or nail had been inserted it broke. This seemed inconceivable at first. These nails were very sturdy. It was simply incomprehensible that a frail old lady could break a strong, one-eighth- of-an-inch-thick steel plate.

On one occasion, after removing a plate, he took it down to the hospital laboratory and tried to break it again in a different place. He put the plate in a vice and tried to hit it with a hammer. It bent with difficulty to an angle of 90° but wouldn't break. It was time to put the thinking cap on.

This mystery went unsolved for some years. That the answer was found shows how many disciplines were then being incorporated in the specialty of orthopaedics. Research in various parts of England finally came up with an intriguing explanation. The cause of the fracture of the plates was due to electro-corrosion caused by using screws made of a metal different from that of the plate. Ions of one metal would move to the other. In effect a small electric cell or battery was formed in the body. Electrolysis was set up and a part of the plate gradually eroded. It eventually broke so a complete re-tooling was necessary. All metals had to be the same.

This included instruments. A screwdriver used on a screw of a different metal could cause electrolysis. Putting a carbide tip on the screwdriver solved this problem. Armed with all these valuable (if basic) pieces of information, science moved ahead. It was eventually found to be more satisfactory to replace the dead head of the femur with an artificial one. At first plastic was used. It worked well for a while but was too soft and wearing took place. Plastic was then replaced by metal, which was much more durable and satisfactory. Similar improvements were steadily made in design and in other features.

In those patients who had an arthroplasty performed on their hips, care had to be taken during the period after the operation. Some of them became so relieved to be finally free of pain that they plunged headlong into over-energetic activities and ended up with other kinds of problems. One patient became so ecstatic that she started a vast array of exercises and developed acute heart failure and died. Malachy could only conclude that sometimes joy can also kill.

Such tragic fates, of course, didn't befall the vast majority of these people. They gradually got the stiffness and rust of years out of their systems. The contracted tissues around the joint began to stretch and become flexible. The muscles began to contract more powerfully, the circulation started to surge and pump again.

He wasn't directly involved in this research. He simply put into practical use each new discovery. He then saw the steady improvement in results. (A number of years later, when he went back to visit his old hospital, he decided to check out the chronic orthopaedic ward. Amazingly, it was empty. It was now being used for a different purpose. He was informed that all the hip cases had been operated on and new artificial hips inserted. All were walking. Some were playing games, others had taken on various types of work. The times they were a-changing.)

During his stay in this hospital there was no need to look for business. Surgical operations took place three times a week and on average eight major procedures would be performed at each session. A surgeon had an operating theatre to himself on fixed days of the week and wasn't interrupted by anyone else. The same team worked together – surgeon, assistant, anaesthetist and a nurse trained in orthopaedics – in all matters relating to this kind of practice, which gave any young surgeon the in-depth experience and back-up he or she needed to perfect their craft. This entailed some mighty discipline.

Nothing, for example, that was due for implantation in the patient's tissues was touched by human hand. The surgeon never fingered the wound. The purpose of this was to avoid infecting bones and joints or damaging tissues. It was called the 'no touch' technique. It was hard to adhere to, or even learn. Many hands tended to want to get in on the act, but bone or joint infection was a mortal blow to an arthroplasty. Great care was taken to avoid it. Any breach of the aseptic barrier was a defeat of the objectives of the operation: a painless, free-moving joint. It was a one-time chance.

There were two out-patient clinics a week. About thirty people on average would be seen on each of these afternoons. Some were reporting back after previously performed operations. They were assessed. Did the operation help them? Had they any complaints?

He realised he had to be careful with his opening questions to a patient. To say at first, 'What are you complaining about?' would often elicit the response, 'I'm not complaining, doctor.' The patients didn't want to be regarded as Moaning Minnies – justifiably. Likewise, the first few minutes of examining them was crucial in building up their trust. He was all too well aware that if he 'foot-faulted' it would come back to haunt him. The old saying 'First impressions last' was eminently sound.

That these people were afraid of pain and kept, so to speak, a beady eye on it, was often made clear to him. He had many patients who wanted stiff joints made more mobile, but when he then informed them that such mobility would have the side effect of pain, they chose to leave matters as they were. It was a question of swings and roundabouts. Every action caused a reaction. Different people had different priorities. Did they wish to grasp the nettle or hold back? Maybe it depended on the job they had, or their threshold of pain.

It began to strike him that the body was in many ways like an old car. It was very difficult to keep it from creaking, especially if it had a lot of miles on the clock. Patients went to people like him for a 'service', but often didn't like what they heard. An oil change (i.e. a blood transfusion) might have been acceptable, but what about having to get a new overhead camshaft? Or a re-bored engine?

Bodies, like cars, didn't run forever. All of them eventually ran out of juice. You could trade in your old jalopy for a new one, but, sadly, humans were stuck with their human chassis, for better or worse. If a red light came on the dashboard it was a signal to act, but how many people just kept on motoring until their engine seized up?

14

The embattled surgeon now took up a new job in Leeds, armed with hope and experience. And a burning desire to find the key to the mystery of pain.

The University Hospital in Leeds stood aloof and proud, detached from its less-eminent institutions. It wasn't a work-a-day place. Indeed, it wasn't too interested in treating the mundane and ordinary. It did, however, throw its many great resources into solving medical and surgical difficulties. The latter had arisen in peripheral hospitals. (Some would say they were created by them).

These were the lost causes. They were unceremoniously dumped on the University Hospital as a final court of appeal. They were the rejects from countless other hospitals. Some were angry, some desperate, some disillusioned. Many had lost confidence in their own hospital. The vast majority, however, came with the assurance that with superior expertise, greater skill and more knowledge their complaints could be studied expertly and a more acceptable solution applied. He thought he could rise to the challenge. He had always been drawn to the hard luck case. A problem, he told himself, was only an opportunity in its workclothes.

As he surveyed the field, he thought it promised a rich harvest. He could feel the scent of discovery in his nostrils. The quarry lurked ahead. He felt he was involved in a chase. The going was hard but the potential prize great. He mentally applied the spur and rein to himself. Where other people merely saw pain, he saw a red light. He was determined to find out what turned it on.

One of his patients was a world class ballerina. She complained of pain in her right groin when she performed but pressed on despite it. The problem was that the pain showed in her performance. To the cruel and penetrating eye of her choreographer, if not audience members, she was missing the timing of a beat. There was a disrupted rhythm in her dance which was like a sword of Damocles hanging above her career.

The cause of her pain couldn't be identified. The common thinking was that she was pushing herself too hard but the opposite could also have been the case. Maybe she was restraining herself for fear of doing damage to those heavily-insured feet.

She was eventually advised to change her career. She wanted to go on but her sponsors weren't prepared to take that risk. He knew that, like all divas, she would have preferred to dance through the pain barrier but he didn't think it would be the right thing to do. He felt she could have more pleasure, and longevity, dancing for her own pleasure away from the footlights. It was a question of damage limitation. Or art versus science. He admitted his was a biased opinion that was from the 'stitch in time saves nine' school of thought. In the end it came down to money, the final arbiter in so many circumstances both inside and outside medicine.

As his ballerina floated off to pastures new – and infinitely quieter – he surveyed the current state of play inside the medical world. It was a time of much ferment. Tuberculosis had just been cured after being a death sentence to so many for so long. The hospitals that had treated it were closing at the rate of knots. Sanatoria were going out of business forever, the racks and frames that had once been their mainstay being dismantled forever. Poliomyelitis had also been conquered. What other mountain was there for a researcher for climb?

Just one, perhaps. The perennial pain slope.

This seemed to be the only defiant, unsubdued force around. In the places where the sanatoria had been, pain clinics started to sprout. Psychiatrists also started to weigh in with their ten cents worth of theorising, turning their fury on the patients in their care. 'It's all in your head,' they said, so many Job's comforters.

Healers from left field also heard the discord and rode over the hill of pain like the Seventh Cavalry. They posited as many theories as the purses of their patients would permit. A fair number of quacks also warmed their hands at the fire. A brace of acupuncturists even came out of the woodwork, reinventing ancient Chinese remedies. Then there were the herbalists and New Age psycho-babblers, ligging on the backs of trendy American panaceas. Straw-clutchers visited everyone from palm-readers to kinesiologists. Everybody, it seemed, had something to offer, desperate situations requiring desperate remedies – but fast. Oliver Pritchett seemed to sum it all up with a kind of wry irony when he wrote: 'One of the most pleasing sounds of springtime to be heard all over the countryside is the contented cooing of osteopaths as men pick up their garden spades.' It was an ill wind, to be sure.

For Malachy Smyth MD, however, a different set of priorities held rein at Leeds University Hospital, where people didn't either have the money or the inclination to seek 'alternative' remedies for their plight.

Some patients arrived on stretchers because they had a form of paralysis, or simply a broken bone which refused to heal. They were all referred from another hospital or another doctor. All were at the end of their tether. They took great care to explain what was the nature of their complaint. They had a lot of practice in doing this as most of them had had many examinations previously. They emphasised that they had difficulty in getting across their point. The other doctors were too busy to listen to long stories and they themselves lacked the skills to describe their symptoms succinctly.

Some of them were hopeless cases but many were also cured by Malachy and his colleagues. Everything seemed to be in the roll of the dice. There but for the clutch of luck went we all. The creaking gate could go on forever, while a healthy young turk could be struck down in his prime. There was no logic to it.

Many of his patients were genuine mysteries. He had two cases of intense burning pain localised to a spot as small as a pinhead but without any sign of abnormality. There was no swelling, nothing to see, nothing to touch. Some cases of pain caused extreme muscle spasm, so severe as to cause the back to be arched so dramatically that the shoulders almost came down to the hips. Some patients had no pain when they were resting, but upon walking developed severe discomfort in their calves. Some had no history of back problems but upon doing something as innocuous as reaching for a cup of coffee one day, felt the kind of intense agony that suggested somebody was stabbing them with a knife. Once again it was Dr Smyth's old friend, the lower back.

On the other side of the scale there were cases where the pain only came on when the patient relaxed. There were some instances where pain was felt at the tip of the spine when the patient sat on a soft chair but was relieved by sitting on a hard chair. People appeared to be buffeted by it from all sides.

One day a young lady of 25 was ushered into his consulting-room. He was familiar with her intriguing story. He knew from her file that she was impeccably healthy but she had an intensely frustrating lower right leg problem. Was it pain or not? She complained of aching and a burning sensation just above the outer side of the left ankle. It began about four years before without any apparent cause. She never injured her leg, nor was it bruised or burnt. She had a lot of aching in her foot too. She couldn't wear stockings nor could she bear to have even a bedsheet touch this part of her leg at night.

After enduring the condition for a while, she went to her doctor. He thought it was a sprain or strain of some kind and that time would heal it. But it didn't. She was referred for a surgical opinion. After X-rays and tests a surgeon excised a sebaceous cyst from her leg. It gave no relief. The cyst had been just living quietly in the area but was blamed for the crime. She was directed to a foot doctor. True to his craft he raised her arches and lowered them, but could never quite get the right height. All was of no avail. Deducing that there was no real physical reason for her complaint, he referred her to a psychiatrist. She went, much against her will, only because she was prepared to try anything that might help. From his astute assessment she was considered normal. (This helped her because it confirmed her own opinion about herself.) She was more determined now than ever not to rest till she got an explanation she could accept.

Everyone was as baffled as she was, and yet when the answer was found it came with a suddenness that startled.

A knowledgeable and erudite dermatology specialist who was a friend of Malachy's examined the patient in question. After doing so he said simply, 'I know what her problem is'. He explained that there was almost certainly a rare benign tumour at the site of the complaint. Her symptoms confirmed him in this diagnosis. The cure was surgical removal.

Malachy pointed out that she'd had an operation in the area and nothing was found. 'They missed it,' the dermatologist said, 'It must be localised to a millimetre. It's only the size of a pinhead.' That afternoon Malachy mapped out an area on the patient's leg with radial lines all intersecting at a central point. That point was very small but it was the centre of intense and exquisite skin tenderness. The following day in the operating theatre he marked out an area of skin, made an incision through the tissue to the bone and removed all *en bloc*. He probably didn't need to be so radical but he wanted to be doubly sure. A few days later the pathologist informed him that he'd found a glomus cell tumour in the specimen he'd sent from the operating theatre. This was great news. It meant he'd been successful.

He went to tell her at once but she wasn't unduly surprised because all her symptoms had disappeared since the operation. She could touch the area without pain and could also let a sheet rest on the affected left leg with impunity.

She was momentarily relieved, but refused to believe she was cured. The emotion that dominated at first was one of fear, fear that it was all a mirage and that she had to brace herself for the worst. Had the operation been a failure she probably would have had a mental breakdown.

A few months later, however, when the symptoms still stayed away, she allowed herself the (for her) luxury of relief. Years of intense worry were banished. She became ecstatic.

The word glomus comes from the Latin meaning ball. The tumour is benign and grows from strange cells that are contractile. They're found at a place where an artery and a vein join. In some cases the tumour assumes a bluish colour when causing pain. It's as if it's giving a flashing signal like the dashboard warnings on one's car. When this happens it's a boon to the patient as its site can be seen. The woman he had treated, however, had suffered from a tumour that was more deeply embedded, which was why it couldn't be seen or felt.

Three other cases of this kind of tumour seen by other physicians in Leeds had different outcomes to that of the 25-year-old lady. Two of them had their legs amputated, with the diagnosis only being made afterwards. The third became suicidal.

Once again it was the luck of the draw.

15

In 1896 a man in Germany fell from a height of a hundred feet. He jumped up immediately, walked thirty steps and then collapsed. He sustained a herniation of a vertebral disc which compressed the spinal cord. He was almost certainly paralysed, but broke no bones.

In 1911 in Scotland a man twisted his back in a slight way. He was immediately paralysed in the legs, having ruptured his vertebral disc, but again no bones were broken.

These are two of the earliest reported cases of 'slipped disc' as the result of injury. The fact that in each case no bones were broken – particularly the first one – demonstrated the fact that discs were wonderful shock absorbers. The two incidents absorbed Malachy.

He now stood right at the orthopaedic frontline, where a relentless war was being fought against pain in the lower back, and indeed all backache. It was the heyday of the aforementioned slipped disc. This was a topic of cocktail party banter. The term seemed to appeal to people. It suggested something tangible and mechanical, something 'out of joint', to use an old and hackneyed phrase. It was familiar to all ears. Most people knew someone who'd slipped a disc. Many people had a close brush with the thing themselves. No one really took it too seriously. It was rather fashionable to have incurred one. It even had a macho connotation. One was out there hacking out an empire. One was ground down on the field of play.

Get-rich-quick opportunists trading on the public's naiveté rushed to put the said disc back in place. There were many disastrous results from such over-zealous manipulations. Some people were even paralysed. Malachy believes no disc ever slipped. He believes it's impossible for it to do so. Ergo, it can't be 'put back'. A totally different mechanism is at work in his view.

Whether caused by a 'slipped disc' or an injury of a more obvious sort, the lower back problem was the one constant at his clinic. It was certain that there would be two or three back patients there every day.

In more cases than not the problem complained of would be tied in with work. It was often implied that the patient in question was, as the saying went, 'pulling a sickie'. Since back problems, or the lack of them, were difficult to prove, it was an ideal excuse for malingerers. Or indeed 'compo culture' merchants. People had trivial car accidents and suddenly developed 'agonising pain' from the fact that another vehicle had crashed into them. They might even develop whiplash as a bonus. Their neck might be put in a brace. They might attend hospital for traction. Some people spent their lives dreaming about such fenderbenders. If one went to an ambulance-chasing lawyer (they advertised now in the Yellow Pages) one could retire for life on the proceeds. It was a bit like winning the Lottery without even buying a ticket.

The obverse side of the coin was that in genuine cases many responsible citizens had indeed 'put out' their backs and as a result had to undergo surgery without any guarantee of success. Their job might also be in danger. If a man agreed to be operated on, he might forego disability compensation, having been deemed to have been 'cured' by the surgery.

In Malachy's view any surgeon contemplating operating on a patient with a back injury can never say for sure that the disc herniation he's suffering from occurred at work. He's also aware that such a patient might well claim he's worse after his operation than before. This places the surgeon between a rock and a hard place.

Court cases arising from such circumstances, he believes, are generally tainted with vested interests.

Events take their course but the claimant (the patient is no longer a patient, he's a 'claimant' on a government form) can't be left forever without a decision on his problem. A compensation hearing is arranged. Lawyers are called in to represent each side. There's usually one for the claimant and one for his employer. The employer's lawyer usually calls in another doctor. His function is to trivialise the claimant's disability. The claimant's doctor, on the other hand, will try to show that the claimant is seriously disabled and incapacitated. The two doctors are thus set on a collision course by the lawyer. By now the case is no longer in any sense a medical one. Litigation has taken over. If the lawyer can convince the presiding judge that a financial settlement is the right one he'll benefit more than anyone else. To this end lawyers try to ensure that doctors will disagree on a given patient. Usually this isn't too hard to do.

In many cases there's no injury but herniation still happens. Patients might be completely immobilised on a frame or in a plaster cast in bed. The scene is thus set with the claimant in limbo, the lawyers in heaven and the doctors in hell. And squabbling.

The settlement award is announced and everyone goes their separate ways. The claimant might now be a patient again. He's got some money but he still has his herniated disc. Maybe he's even lost his job. The doctors get their fees for their day in court but they've lost too. The judge goes home disgruntled after refereeing a financial hassle. He has nothing to show for his efforts because he's on a salary. But the lawyers have few complaints. They've cast themselves in the mode of referees at a prize fight where they pocket the gate receipts while the two fighters (the doctor and patient) both go home empty-handed.

Malachy remains perturbed by this circus of deceit and pocket-lining but it has never been his prime area of enquiry. All through his life he's been at pains (if that's not the wrong expression in the circumstances) to stress that science has never established that a herniated disc can cause sciatica. It's always been suspected that this is so but it can't be proven scientifically.

A broken leg, he says, is straightforward. It can't be mimicked. But an apocryphal back injury can. One condition can be diagnosed objectively, the other can't. A man who says 'That hurts,' has to be taken at his word when talking about something as hard to pin down as sciatic pain. Some men, lazy or just plain cunning, undoubtedly used sciatica as an excuse to go on the dole. It was almost a failsafe mechanism for easy money. In the old days, snake oil salesmen pawned off substandard goods on patients but in these instances it was the patient who was selling the doctor the snake oil. And many fell for it, performing all forms of tests on non-existent maladies. In such cases, the 'pain' miraculously disappeared as soon as the malingerer in question received his juicy cheque. Filthy lucre, in such instances, was a more effective painkiller than any anaesthetist could provide.

He realises that this sad state of affairs has made surgeons reluctant to perform surgery for fear of being sued for negligence. It's also led to a dramatic increase in the number of detectives employed by insurance companies. Such detectives are delegated to spy on claimants to try and find out if they're as immobilised as they claim. One person he heard about was 'crippled' in a wheelchair by day but out tripping the light fantastic in discotheques by night. Another one was unable to bend until one day the detective called at his door impersonating a ticket-seller. When it came time to sign the ticket that was sold, the detective 'accidentally' dropped his pen and, bingo, the crippled man promptly bent down to pick it up like somebody in the full of his health.

The nefarious malingerer was caught on camera doing this, the detective's ally being in the nearby bushes with his camcorder, or maybe upstairs in a building across the street with a long-range lens. Other people who might be caught on camera would be those who 'rehearsed' their falls in the toilets of shopping malls and hamburger joints. Once CCTV footage of such nasty 'accidents' on wet floors comes to light, the claims for damages are suddenly withdrawn from court.

Malachy doesn't dwell unduly on anecdotes like this. Since he has devoted the better part of his life to pain relief, he prefers to think that people who tell him they're suffering really are. Once you lose trust in your patient you may as well call it a day. But having said that, a man who came into his surgery limping on the 'wrong' foot, or who entered the Wimbledon tennis championships the same week he developed a dodgy spine, would have found himself getting short shrift from the pioneering doctor.

He said some years ago: 'When I started orthopaedic practice, I believed completely all my patient told me about his pain. When I finished, he had to prove he had pain before I could treat him. The lawyer has been successful in destroying trust. It was a pyrrhic victory.' The reason it was pyrrhic is that in our litigious, grasping age, surgeons will shy away from life-saving operations for fear of a massive legal claim even if they feel the purported surgery has a great chance of success. Surely it's the patient who loses out in this scenario.

Lower back pain is one of the most devious and unpindownable forms of discomfort. Many people make their living by trying to treat it, both from the traditional and alternative sides of the medical fence. Patients part with copious sums of money to eradicate their pain, often unwisely. Scores of books on the subject have also been published, many of them contradicting the theories of the one before. Because we can't see pain as an entity on an X-ray, the way is open for anyone to put forward a hypothesis and run with it. Some people are healed as a result of such hypotheses but many more gullible ones are exploited.

Neither is there any guarantee that what worked for A will work for B. There are as many types of pain as there are people, and as time goes on doctors are beginning to see the huge effect one's personality has on how one deals with pain. It could also be deemed responsible for actually causing it, either partially or fully. We could even go so far as to say pain is as specific to the sufferer as his or her DNA.

All of us are subject to 'wear and tear' on our back, and most of us suffer lower back pain at some time of our lives, but if the pain is chronic or persistent we would usually have something done about it. If our disc bulges or the shell breaks, fluid can leak out of it, resulting in herniation. If it leaks onto a nerve, the pain can be excruciating.

Herniated discs don't always cause pain, however. Some magnetic resonance imagining (MRI) studies have revealed bulges where the patient in question has no pain, as did some CAT scans. Alternatively, one could have a bulge in one's disc and suffer no pain at all. There are no absolute laws, which is why there's so much room for conjecture in this area – and exploitation.

One writer said pinpointing back pain was similar to trying to identify 'the one person who's booing in an entire stadium of spectators'. If the body is a network, which it is, lower back pain is the elusive short-circuit.

It's a well-known fact that some people seem to be able to train their minds to 'postpone' pain, like the woman rushing into a burning house to rescue her child, only falling to the ground in semi-consciousness after the immediate danger is averted. In a minor way, we might see the same pattern in somebody running a marathon and having reached 'the wall', i.e. the point at which their system has, as it were, run out of batteries, but they still manage to get that extra juice from somewhere for the surge to the finishing line.

Are these people operating on some kind of reserve psychological petrol tank? Are they in some way like those samurai warriors who seem to be able to withstand tortuous pain as they enter TM-like states? Or, more obviously, like the people who dance on hot coals for the delectation of tourists in foreign countries? We've heard of sports people 'playing through the pain barrier' in important Cup ties, again 'delaying' their agony until the final whistle. Is this equivalent to the provincial headless chicken still in motion after its decapitation?

In a sense all pain is retrospective. If we take the simple analogy of hitting our thumb with a hammer, there's a milli-second where we know it's going to sting like hell but hasn't begun to yet. Is this the milli-second it takes for our finger to 'tell' the brain it's been hit? One might have imagined pain sensors would travel down the nerve pathway more speedily than this.

Patients suffering from acute or chronic pain often say to doctors, 'Please don't tell me it's all in my head'. The implication is that if he does they'll be seen as fraudulent. Nothing could be further from the truth because all pain has a psychological element. This doesn't mean we're responsible for it, merely that our personality probably dictates its ferocity and/or duration. That's why we speak of some people having greater pain thresholds than others. This doesn't mean we've 'caused' the pain. Rather we monitor it, albeit unconsciously. The mind-body duality gives rise to a chicken-and-egg situation. The same physical root may result in person A feeling agony and person B only feeling mildly uncomfortable, or evincing no reaction at all.

The bottom line is that most sensations are largely a function of our anticipation of them. Fear intensifies pain just as excitement intensifies pleasure. (Witness Pavlov's dogs salivating when they hear the food bell.) The foretaste dictates just how pleasurable or painful the 'taste' is going to be. In a word, pain is a habit – and this is exemplified in the back perhaps more than in any other area of our anatomy, which is why its study has become such a bone (excuse the pun) of contention among those who purport to heal it.

16

One day while Malachy was doing his rounds in the hospital he was startled by a cry of agony which came from a bed further down the ward. He asked the nurse accompanying him what was wrong with the patient in question.

'Terminal cancer,' she replied. 'He's asking for his next injection. He's heavily medicated because he has a lot of pain.'

On further inquiry Malachy found that the man had had an operation for cancer of the bladder a few years before. The procedure was considered successful then. His cancer had, however, recurred and was now involving this precise area. The patient was having severe pain in the lower part of his back and one leg. He was now confined to bed. Malachy asked the doctor if he could examine him. 'Certainly,' he said, but added, 'The cancer has spread to the spine, There's nothing more we can do for him.'

Malachy checked his X-rays and then examined him. Apart from solid clinical evidence of nerve root irritation, he could find no other abnormality. He was sixty years of age and in good health otherwise but the effects of the pain were gradually draining away his energy and his will to live.

He didn't survive much longer. At the post-mortem Malachy asked that the pathologist scrutinise the lower spinal dural canal. He did so. Two small cancer nodules had infiltrated the nerve sheath of the great nerve running to the leg. Malachy was touched with remorse. He was positive that these two small nodules had caused all of the poor man's misery. He couldn't prove it but he knew it was true.

What bothered him in addition to the normal human response of sorrow for a fellow man was the tunnel vision of the people caring for him, which worked under the assumption that because he had cancer, pain anywhere was almost accepted as axiomatic. There was also the subtext that, considering he was a terminal patient, what point would there be in doing any form of investigation?

He went home that night with a lump in his throat. He was disappointed in his colleagues but also in himself. Maybe he needed to push his points further, to have a bigger voice. Lucy told him he needed to unwind. At times like this she was his safety valve. Every doctor brought his work home to some extent, but there had to be a cut-off point. If you became too involved with your patients you ran the risk of being unable to cope when tragedy struck. It was a thin line between sympathy and empathy.

At what point did Malachy Smyth become 'The Doctor'? At what point did he turn back again? How could you go home to watch a light-hearted television programme and turn your mind off totally from the sick and the senile? Some members of his profession had that facility but he hardly envied them for it.

People think doctors have an immunity to death because they see so much of it, he says, but nothing could be farther from the truth. They might develop certain strategies to deal with it, but that doesn't mean it hits them any easier than the rest of us. Malachy remembers every patient he lost, some with more emotion than others, but it never stops hurting. Neither does it ever become automatic, or expected. He can't predict his reaction to a given loss any more than the proverbial man in the street can. He wasn't given immunity to tragedy with his medical degree. He knows we're all in this particular furnace together.

Neither would he ever fall into the 'sin' of certitude. The only thing you know for sure is that you know nothing for sure. Some 'terminal' cases survived, while twenty-year-olds walked under a bus after getting a clear bill of health from their GP, or developed some enigmatic symptom that turned into a potentially lethal condition. Life was a lottery. All he could do was his best, using whatever technology that was at his disposal. Sometimes he felt he was going up the down staircase, but he always felt that if he stuck to his basic beliefs, maybe, just maybe, he might get the results he was looking for.

By now he had developed an obsession with pain and its alleviation. He decided to do some experiments on his patients to further his research. Over the next five years he operated on fifty of them, each with a herniated disc. Such patients were selected very carefully. All of them had to be between 20 and 25 years old and only first-time herniations were considered for the project. Anyone with a legal case pending wasn't deemed eligible for fear of the deceit factor entering in.

The nature of the experiment was carefully explained to each patient. They could refuse to go ahead if they wished. All of them were warned of possible complications and even danger. They were told, for instance, that they could be paralysed and perhaps have a weak foot or leg afterwards. It was impressed on them that this was the first time such research had ever been done. He admitted to them that he himself was in the dark too and therefore couldn't forecast or guarantee anything. All they could be assured of was that he would take no risks.

Out of a series of twenty two patients, eight were chosen for the first testing. The site of the skin incision was mapped out so that it would be exactly over that of the disc herniation, deep inside the spinal canal.

He removed the disc in each case. At this point the actual operation was over. The patient could have been sewn up and bandaged and then taken to the recovery room. But because his interest lay in proving that the pain was caused by the bulging disc on the nerve, this wasn't done. Instead, before closing the patient's surgical wound, the missing disc was replaced by a nylon loop which passed under the nerve at the same site the disc had pressed on. Both ends of the loop were then brought up the tunnel to the surface before the wound was closed. He now had a nerve root with a nylon loop around it, the ends of which were protruding through the skin incision. The nylon was round a large nerve root called the first sacral root. It contained most of the nerve fibres that went to the leg muscles.

It could easily be seen that if the slack in the nylon was taken up, the loop in the spinal cord would come into contact with the nerve root. It would actually press on the nerve at the same time the disc had done.

After the first operation the patient returned to his room. Thankfully there hadn't been any complications. The following day the sciatic pain in his leg was completely gone. He was quite pleased with this. Malachy told him that the operation had been a success. He also told him that the testing that would constitute his research would be done two days later.

Nobody knew what to expect, least of all the researcher himself. It was possible that the patient's heart would react to the sudden nerve stimulus. It could even stop. He might be thrown into a convulsive seizure.

Two days later, as planned, the research started.

The dressing over the wound in the lower part of the patient's back was removed. The two ends of nylon stuck through the wound like two antennae. Malachy grasped both of them and took up the slack. Nothing happened. He increased the pressure. At once the patient jumped and said he felt pain. Malachy asked, 'Is it just in the skin?' 'No,' the patient replied, 'It's deep in my spine. It's my old pain coming back!'

Malachy relaxed traction on the nylon and the pain, in turn, disappeared completely. The patient was relieved. He calmed down as it became obvious that no great calamity was going to occur. Malachy pilled a little stronger and the pain spread from the back into the back of the leg. It also increased in severity. He felt he was onto something. It was unfathomable to him that he could produce pain and then stop it at will. He did it again and again. Once the patient knew the pain could be stopped on command, he had no fear of it.

82

It occurred to Malachy that he might be able to measure pain by the pressure required to produce it, and then to put a figure on its severity by the length it travelled. That, however, was for the future. The nylon was removed simply by pulling on one end and slipping it out. It was a moment of triumph. Pain could be started and stopped at will in seconds.

The patient in question was also enthralled at this spectacle. 'We now have pain by the scruff of the neck,' Malachy said, to which he replied, 'Give me a hold of that nylon thread so I can give Mr Pain the hell he gave me for so many years.' Malachy lengthened the nylon so he could grasp it. He then gave him a rod to hold so that he could point out the part of his leg where the pain was when there was tension on the nylon. The patient pulled it and felt the pain travelling down his leg. He then began beating his leg as if the pain was something live travelling under his skin. After he stopped pulling, the pain stopped. He had, quite literally, 'killed' it.

Malachy went to bed that night with a 'eureka' feeling. After all the years of struggle, he seemed to be finally cracking the nut.

As far as the patient was concerned, he had no ill-effects from the experiment. His sciatic pain was completely relieved. He was able to go home in a week. Malachy marked in indelible black ink the path the pain followed when the nerve was stimulated. It was about two inches wide. It started at the middle of the buttock area, passed down the middle of the back of the thigh and swept around the outer side of the calf. The inky path was still plainly to be seen when the patient was leaving the hospital. Malachy told him not to wash it off.

He was seen again two weeks later. He had no pain, but the black pain highway was still clearly marked. As Malachy ran his finger along it, testing for any abnormality, he said, 'There's no traffic on that road anymore. You better get your local highway department to close it down completely. It will only attract the wrong kind of traveller.'

Over the next four years his explorations continued. He carried out over a hundred operations. He tested the same nerve in all his patients to make sure the first one wasn't just an accident. Identical results were obtained in all eight cases. He then turned to all the other nerves in the lumbar spine on one side. A pain pathway for each of these was mapped out on the leg.

When the pathway for all the nerves was put on to it, it looked like a surveyor's map. You could look at an area on the map and know at once which area of the spine was represented.

A nerve in the upper chest region of the spine was stimulated in the same way. It was the fourth root. This nerve was extremely sensitive. Merely touching it resulted in excruciating, unbearable pain. It was beyond the patient's endurance to touch it again. The pain in the lower part of the spine was nothing by comparison.

He tried other tests to assimilate new data. In three patients with the nylon loop around the nerve, but only taut enough to touch it without pain, the leg with the straight knee was raised from the couch. When it was raised to about twenty-five degrees, pain began to spread into the leg from the back. It was inferred that the nerve itself began to move at this point. The same thing was done to one of the patients where the nerve roots were widely exposed during his operation. The lower roots moved up and down with each leg movement. They looked like pulleys as they flapped up and down and in and out. These movements resembled very closely those of the tendons on the back of the hand when the fingers bent and straightened. The nerves then had considerable laxity and freedom of movement.

All of the soft tissues in the region of the nerve roots were tested to see if pain could be caused by pulling on them or straining them. Only one showed evidence of sensitivity. This was the structure binding the vertebral bones together, through which a disc herniates. Traction on it caused backache.

Electrodes were inserted in muscles of the thigh and leg while the nerve root was being stimulated by the nylon loop. No spasm was caused. It was taken for granted that the cramp in the muscles of the leg didn't cause pain.

There are two small joints on each side of the vertebral bone, the so-called facet joints. He didn't test the capsule which surrounds them to see if there was evidence of sensitive nerve fibres in them. However, by a process of elimination and deduction, there seemed no doubt that they were very sensitive.

'A patient,' says Malachy, 'tilts and rotates his spine to free the nerve root from the protruding disc. In doing so, he strains the small joints at the sides of the vertebral bone. This in turn causes severe pain in these small joints. The great muscles of the back then go into spasm to protect them.'

This causes the classical hunched up appearance of the patient with a 'bad' back, who's often a figure of fun for cartoonists, being drawn with arrow sparks coming out of the painful area. These small joints don't usually cause this very painful spasm unless they're inflamed by overuse – or unaccustomed use. This condition, he points out, can be completely independent of a herniated disc. It can occur on its own.

The pain is more severe than sciatica. Strangely, the condition is less serious than that of disc herniation but more incapacitating while it lasts.

A gelatinous material bulges backwards from between the two lower vertebral bones. It's about the size of the tip of the index finger. If it touches the nerve root just behind it, pain is caused and eventually passes down the leg. It's then called sciatica.

His experiments proved that this does, in fact, happen. It hadn't been proven before. It was, however, assumed. If the direction of this protrusion is such that it misses the nerve root, nobody is any the wiser.

When this apparently simple circumstance occurs it sets in motion a train of events which spread in diverse directions. If it's in a worker, he probably loses his job. The footballer loses his place on the team. The professional golfer abandons his career, and the employer is subjected to many difficulties. It costs insurance companies a lot of money. It presents governments with well-nigh insoluble problems. It recalls Aesop's Fable: All for the want of a nail, the shoe was lost.

Malachy regrets this is so. He believes the term herniated disc should be abandoned, and so should that of slipped disc. The disc neither herniates nor slips. The term herniated disc conjures up a major catastrophe in people's minds. Action is taken and attitudes adopted on an emergency basis.

He suggests a diagnosis of 'cartilage cyst in a vertebral joint' instead. Treatment would be removal of the cyst using an operating endoscope. The patient would be in hospital for a very short time. In most cases he could return to work in a few days, depending on his job. There should be no permanent disability.

There are other back conditions which, he feels, should be treated accordingly. As he often says, we constantly hear the phrase 'He has a bad back', but the phrase 'He has a bad stomach' is rarely heard. Where the latter is concerned, other diagnoses are attached. One may have gallstones, appendicitis, colitis, gastritis, gastric ulcer, even constipation. It's regarded almost as an insult to be told that all you've got is constipation, and yet it's a condition which has to be medically treated, even if we feel we can't tell anyone about it!

The back, he insists, should be treated with the same concern as the abdomen. Most back sufferers are given an ugly-looking corset. They hang it up at the back of the kitchen door and only wear it when they're keeping the next doctor's appointment. The problem with 'bad backs' is that neither an X-ray nor laboratory can make a diagnosis in many of these cases. The informed human input is still needed. This is hard work but it can mean the difference between being totally incapacitated by intolerable pain or being at home free of it.

Malachy removed one herniated disc in an unusual manner, by having his patient in what he calls the 'knee chest' position on the operating table. He was sitting on his heels with his feet over the edge. His stomach was on his thighs and his forehead on the table. It was the same position Muslims adopt when they pray. Its practical advantage for Malachy was that it made the disc more accessible to him. He learned it from a Manchester surgeon but doesn't know of anyone else who has used it. When a colleague saw the anaesthetised patient crouching like this, he commented on the fact that it was a Muslim praying position. 'I'll take help from anywhere I can get it!' the resourceful surgeon replied.

17

Malachy's research work was eventually published in *The Journal of Bone and Joint Surgery*. He was asked by the journal's editor, William Rogers, how many reprints he'd like. 'Seven or eight,' he suggested. Rogers advised him to have at least 300 done.

He was inundated with letters as a result. These came from major world centres of research and from the elite teaching hospitals and universities. They all wanted reprints of the article. Many wanted more information. Some wanted fine points clarified. One or two wanted to pick a fight. One writer was a disbelieving Thomas, asserting that sciatic pain was not, and could not, be caused the way he had described.

Most of the requests for reprints had an individual letter attached. Other requests were from journals and book publishers. None of these expressions of interest contained a stamped addressed envelope, he was disappointed to see.

To mail the reprints alone cost him a lot of money. The effort to do so cost more. He wasn't supported by a grant or foundation. The expense was his alone. Only a few recipients wrote notes of thanks.

He sent a reprint to the editor of a leading orthopaedic journal. He wasn't asked to do so. This journal had rejected his work for publication. At the time he suspected the snub wasn't against the article but rather the department from which it emanated. Publication in a prestigious journal meant more authority and influence to the institution concerned. The then-editor, a practicing orthopaedic surgeon, wanted that influence for his own institution. His desire, thankfully, was thwarted, because the article was later published in an even more prestigious journal.

Malachy's medical college didn't ask him for a reprint. A prophet wasn't accepted in his own country. His alma mater, however, found out about it. St. Mary's capitalised a little on it and attributed the success to their excellent teaching. He didn't begrudge them this. Later he got a letter from the headmaster informing him they were hanging a picture of him in the school hall. He was to be a role model.

He didn't welcome this onerous responsibility. The very thought was worrisome. The pictures they had hanging on the wall, he remembered, were forbidding. He dreaded seeing his own visage glowering among them. As a schoolboy he had always felt the eyes of the men in these photographs followed him wherever he went. Now if he re-visited his old college he faced the prospect of being haunted by his own shadow, a rather unappetising prospect to say the least.

His appointment in Leeds was due to end in a year, an eventuality that also caused him some concern. He knew it was going to be difficult securing a permanent post as an orthopaedic surgeon. Medicine had become nationalised while he was on active duty in the Armed Services, with the result that there was very little private practice now. One had to be appointed by a board of doctors.

These were mostly men who had managed by skill and cunning not to don a uniform. They were now in charge of appointments to permanent posts in the health service. They preferred to appoint other doctors who hadn't served in these posts. They didn't really want ex-servicemen around them because they found them disconcerting. Birds of a feather stuck together. As a result the doctor returning from the war had to wait a long time, maybe forever, to get a permanent job.

It was a perverse way of 'rewarding' military service. The English, Malachy believes, have a strong streak of Puritanism in them. He notes that the Puritans were said to have banned bear-baiting not because it caused pain to the bear but because it gave pleasure to the spectator. One doctor even accused him of having a gala time in the war while he himself suffered various agonies from his living-room, having borne the affliction of combat in dignified silence.

There was a good deal of undercover work going on at this time, with applicants for jobs quietly seeing board members and getting what they wanted with a nod and a wink. Many permanent appointments were made before boards of doctors even convened meetings. The interview succeeded the appointment. He was reminded of Sir Archibald McIndoe's remark, 'Skill is fine and genius is splendid, but the right contacts are more valuable than either.'

It was the Old Boys Network kicking in with a vengeance. Things would never change. It wasn't what you knew but who you knew. Consultancies were organised on rugby pitches and golf courses – probably in the 19th hole. He knew he could never be a beneficiary of any of this, not being a party animal. Neither would he have wanted to be.

These so-called consultant positions weren't what they implied. The occupants were merely specialists in a particular field of medicine. They were overworked and the pay was poor. There was little scope for enhancing one's income by private practice.

So his training was soon to end, and he faded the prospect of a long wait for a consultancy. However, his published work brought him dividends that completely changed both his life and outlook. Also, out of the blue, he was offered the post of Clinical Research Fellow in Toronto, Canada. This was to last about two years and was (sharp intake of breath) salaried. Things were starting to look up.

He decided he wouldn't return to England. The prospects there looked bleak. He would be a state doctor with constricted freedom, subservient to lay administrators and repetitive, grinding work. Most consultants saw about thirty patients in a morning clinic. Notes had to be written about each one after examination. Patients also had to be seen in the wards, outlying hospitals visited and operations performed. Sometimes six or seven of them would be performed in a morning or afternoon. Then there were fracture clinics, putting on casts and examining X-rays.

There was always a huge crowd at the fracture clinic, which often didn't end till seven o'clock in the evening. In between, to liven things up, there would be emergencies. Everything would have to be dropped for these. Help was limited. Then there were the night calls, just in case you were getting too fond of your beauty sleep after a hectic day, or even (God forbid) starting to think life was actually meant to be enjoyed by putting your feet up.

Lucy feared she would become that common medical phenomenon, a Doctor's Widow, watching the clock each night for his return, but as time went on he developed a routine of work and leisure. He had seen too many colleagues suffer burn-out to set himself up for the same fate.

He had nine months to prepare to leave. It was done on schedule. He arranged for transportation of his furniture and decided to go a few weeks after returning from a last short trip to Paris with Lucy. Soon they were on their way. They had become emigrants.

When he first came to England fifteen years previously it had been the heart of a great empire. Doctors were free to practise as they saw fit, but since the war their wings had been clipped. They had become ground-down figures, and the country itself a small trading nation trailing dim clouds of glory. Lucy and himself left with nostalgia, and the treasured Irish lament for what might have been.

He now won a Research Fellowship in a hospital in Toronto. It was much appreciated. Permanence at last! It was the start of a new decade and hopefully a new phase in his life. But he'd never take anything for granted. All too often in the past he'd been deceived by fool's gold.

They arrived in Toronto in the middle of a torrential thunderstorm, the like of which neither of them had ever witnessed before. It was followed by a clammy humidity which sapped their energy. They also felt incredibly lonely. Their emotional turmoil seemed to be underlined by the freakish weather conditions. Maybe the elements were in sympathy with them.

They spent two years there but they were hardly memorable. Canada, Richard Benner said, 'is a country so square that even the female impersonators are women.' Malachy also found it somewhat boring. It didn't leave much of an impression on him but he concedes that it paved the way for him getting into the U.S., where he would spend many happy years.

18

If you can remember the sixties, they say, you weren't there. For Malachy they passed in a blur of activity. After Canada he spent two years as chief of Orthopaedic Surgery at the Clifton Springs General Hospital in the Finger Lakes area of upper state New York, so called because a number of lakes converge here. Iroquois legend has it that when the 'Great Spirit' laid his hand upon the earth, the impression of his fingers resulted in the spindly pattern of the water. Scientists prefer to put the strange configuration down to the work of glaciers in the Ice Age, but why spoil a perfectly interesting fable with the truth?

Malachy didn't have a licence to practice medicine in America at this time so he had to be 'snuck' in under the wire, as it were, his bosses managing to convince the government they were training him. The opposite was closer to the truth. One of the latter, the Chief Executive, even became one of his patients. He had a persistent back problem caused by a herniated disc. Malachy operated and achieved a successful result, thereby establishing his credibility early. No money exchanged hands, but he suddenly felt very secure in his new post.

Lucy and himself moved into a 2½ acre residence and he also bought a power boat. He spent a lot of time on the water after his workload was completed, nature proving to be the best therapy of all to unwind after a day at the office. He brought Lucy out with him and it was like a second honeymoon. She'd borne with him through all the lean times when doors seemed to keep closing in his face and now they were reaping the harvest for those years of frustration. He felt they deserved it.

The house had a basement bar and Lucy and himself threw parties here to entertain his business friends. Lucy also started painting at this time, doing an impressive one of their boat on Keuka Lake.

Every now and then, when he felt he needed a break, he took her down to Florida to play golf and swim, leaving his patients to be taken care of by a colleague. The months from December to March were the ones he preferred for such breaks. Otherwise it was unbearably hot and dry, and all one tended to see were retired people sunning themselves. (Con Houlihan once said, 'Florida is a place where everybody goes to bed early to preserve their energy for sitting round the pool the next day.') He bought some real estate but never contemplated living there full time.

He started a private orthopaedic practice in Utica, also in upper state New York, at this time. He kept his Clifton Springs house but sold his boat for a tidy sum. He had bought it for $10,000 but at the time of selling it it had appreciated to a cool $200,000. At that kind of profit margin, maybe he should have chucked in the medicine and become a nautical speculator.

Some of his patients at this time were ladies of the night who were suffering from broken hips. They weren't exactly monied and he often operated on them for free. Asked if he was ever offered any other 'favours' for his work, he says, 'No more than a wink'. (One is reminded of the surgeon who, after treating a prostitute for sciatica, informed her as she was leaving the surgery that she would be 'back on her back' in no time!)

One of his colleagues in the Utica practice was a Turkish plastic surgeon who owned a downtown brothel as a sideline. 'That's where the big money is,' he told Malachy, 'and the hours are better too.' Another Turk who worked with him in Clifton Springs believed in polygamy. He said it was in his culture. Both of these men were very easy about their sexuality. There was no guilt involved. Their wives didn't seem unduly bothered about it either.

In Utica Malachy found himself on the staff of no less than three hospitals. He was the only orthopaedist trained to do total hip surgery. At this time surgeons were prohibited from putting any foreign material into the body: a ludicrous caveat dating back to an old federal law which left American medicine back in the Stone Ages *vis-à-vis* its British counterparts. Malachy himself was even accused of practising 'experimental' surgery, a smear that could have damaged his career had America not finally caught up with Europe in this regard.

Reason eventually prevailed and the law was repealed. Surgeons now travelled in great numbers to places like London and Manchester to learn the finer points of hip replacement, By this time, alas, many Americans had undergone many years of needless pain. Some, too, were too old and infirm to have the surgery that would have improved the quality of their lives immeasurably.

This was the first time he had run a practice on his own and it was something of a culture shock for him. So was America itself. Its ways were very different to anything he'd experienced before. One was given a lot of power but also expected to deliver the goods. The atmosphere was laidback.

In his first week he contacted a medical equipment store to furnish his office. It was no sooner said than done. So fast in fact that he hadn't the money ready for the furnisher. When he told him this, the man replied 'Don't worry; it's yours for nothing. Your office is a valuable display window for us. The furniture is far more valuable to me in your office than in my store'. Rugged individualism had come to Utica! Out of such ingenuity was capitalism built. He certainly wasn't complaining. Only in years to come would the rest of the world wake up to the importance of what has come to be called product endorsement.

Two months later his practice was thriving, free furniture notwithstanding. More and more patients were coming in. But he noticed that his bank account was in the red. There was a shortfall in the patients' payments to him so he phoned up his bank manager and told him he was having cash flow problems.

'How much do you need, doc?' the manager asked. 'About $500,' he replied. 'Oh you need more than that,' the manager persisted, whereupon he gave him an advance of $2,000. It was so different to the British way. This wasn't an overdraft; rather a raising of his account to the level of that amount.

In 1962 he took up a post at the Workers' Compensation Board (WCB) in New York. He had an office on the 47th floor of the World Trade Centre: one of the Twin Towers that was destroyed on September 11, 2001. His job was to assess degrees of disability among injured employees. He was also made medical director of a rehabilitation unit. Both posts were salaried. He was sent to New York to do a year's course on compensation law. Lucy and himself being given an apartment in Gramercy Park. They spent four days here every week, then flew home to Utica at the weekends. He also operated on Saturday mornings. It was a hectic but fulfilling period of his life.

The varying posts he secured all had their perks. The WCB contract and one of his hospital posts both came with courtesy cars. Considering both he and Lucy also had their own personal ones as well, that meant at one point there were four cars in his driveway. America was certainly the land of opportunity for him. His nomadic life wouldn't have been possible if Lucy had had kids so there was at least this advantage to be had from childlessness.

He got on well with his WCB clients as he always tried to give them a 'fair shake'. Some other doctors could be pernickety, forever arguing about the small print. There was one man in particular who had a bad reputation within the Board and he eventually got his comeuppance. One day a dissatisfied ex-worker, irked at what he perceived to be an insulting pay-out, came into his office armed with a firearm and shot him. The wound wasn't fatal but it sent out a message to everyone about the dangers of their work.

This was America after all, the land of the trigger-happy. It would have been ironic if Malachy himself ended up being disabled as a result of his work on behalf of the disabled.

Another client was a man who was more severely affected than most. In fact he seemed hardly able to stand. He was on two crutches and hobbled up to the stand to plead his case. The requisite sum was duly awarded and Malachy went back to his office, which happened to be a few floors above where the hearing took place. As he looked out the window he saw the man slowly lurching across the street on his crutches.

Then something strange happened. The man was in the middle of a pedestrian crossing when the lights changed to red. Suddenly an avalanche of cars started to speed towards him. Malachy stepped closer to the window, worried suddenly about whether he'd make it to the other side of the street in time.

He needn't have worried. As soon as the would-be cripple saw the cars descending on him he dropped his trusty crutches and broke into a run. Not only was he an athlete: he could have got a job in the Abbey Theatre with his acting ability!

Malachy became a Fellow of the American College of Surgeons (F.A.C.S.) in time. To attain this status, one had to be examined in no less than fifty operations, and also to be recommended by eight surgeons – no mean achievement. He also became an American citizen. Some of his Irish friends didn't succeed in getting the coveted F.A.C.S. and most Irish and British qualifications weren't recognised so they had to go home to look for a permanent post.

One day when he was driving home from work he came upon a traffic accident. A car had crashed into a barrier, stunning the driver but causing much more damage to the female passenger. He had an 'M.D.' tag on his windscreen so was rushed through the crowd of people to where the accident occurred. When he saw the woman his heart missed a beat. She had stopped breathing and her scalp was pulled down over her face. It wasn't a pretty sight. He managed to put the scalp back and stanch the flow of blood with an emergency kit he always carried with him. The ambulance finally arrived and took her to hospital. It's probable he saved her life as she was about to choke on her own blood.

The sixties seemed to breathe new vigour into him. It was a decade of transition, of liberation. All the old cobwebs seemed to have been left behind. The sexual revolution took place, the subdued tensions of a generation bursting forth with music, film and dance. Women also had more freedom because of the pill. It was an era of rebelliousnessness, the kind of rebelliousness people like Elvis Presley and James Dean spearheaded a decade before. 'Make love not war' was the catchphrase of the moment.

Richard Nixon ran for the U.S. Presidency in 1960 and Malachy supported his campaign. (It would be many years before the scandal of Watergate). Nixon promised to give more funds to medical boards and his department was one of them. One day he arrived in to work and the director of his section invited him into his room where there was a safe. Inside it was his salary for a year, all of which had been sent on by Nixon. It was all in crisp fifty dollar bills: a mouth-watering sight.

Nixon didn't succeed in his bid for the presidency at this attempt, being pipped at the post by John F. Kennedy, the fresh-faced young man with the Hollywood-style good looks proving too formidable for the dour, stubbled Republican. He also had Irish roots, and made that historic trip here in 1962.

The good Doctor Smyth might well have alleviated JFK's back pain if he had been approached by him. Kennedy was plagued with this throughout his short life. He hid it from the public but even in some photographs his discomfort is manifest in the rigid stance. He suffered from arthritis too and it was exacerbated during World War II when he spent thirty hours in the freezing cold water of the dark straits of the Solomon Islands after his boat (PT109) was sliced in half by a Japanese destroyer.

'I wasn't a war hero,' Kennedy said self-effacingly after the incident, 'The Japanese simply torpedoed my boat.' He was being humble here. The reality was that he rescued a sailor from drowning and brought him to a nearby island, afterwards swimming to another island where he felt the Japanese wouldn't have had a base. Jack's father Joe was less shy about beefing up the incident and used it to bolster his son's presidential hopes when that prospect loomed up years later.

Kennedy had 'the tough hide of Irish potatoes,' as Inga Arvad, an early lover, put it. His mother Rose averred in similar vein, 'In our family, illness wasn't a big deal. We had a long tradition of it so nobody really complains about it very much.'

Rose was made aware of the fact that Jack was a sickly child almost from birth. He had whooping cough and measles as a child, then scarlet fever, headaches, various abdominal pains and of course Addison's Disease, which was caused by a deficiency of the adrenal glands. This caused his weight to drop alarmingly.

'It's Jackie's cooking!' he joked. He later claimed it was due to the after-effects of a bout of malaria. It gave him a tan complexion, which ironically attracted the ladies. They had no idea of the pain he was in. This was alleviated to some extent by cortisone, a new drug which he referred to as 'a miracle in a syringe'. He frequently injected himself with this, and also took Demerol in large doses. In 1954 he had an operation on his back and suffered a urinary tract infection afterwards, hovering at death's door for a time before he recovered. He also spent some time at the famous Mayo Clinic in Rochester, Minnesota, as indeed would Malachy.

'I don't expect to live much past fifty,' he said once, 'so I'm going to make the most of the time I have.' He certainly did that. To the greater world he was a virile war hero, but in reality he was more a candidate for one of Dr Malachy's disability pensions than a draft card. But then the world also saw him as a devoted husband.

It's amusing to think of him canoodling with Marilyn Monroe, his most famous boudoir conquest, while in the throes of back pain from a problematic disc, either injecting himself with cortisone or stacking up on Demerol. (Ms Monroe would have provided him with some Nembutal, her own drug of choice, if he ran out.)

Less than a year after Kennedy visited Ireland, Malachy was in his clinic one day when his secretary came in to him and said, 'We no longer have a President. He's just been assassinated in Texas.' It was nearly impossible to take in. The world would never be quite the same again.

Not that everybody loved Kennedy unqualifiably. One of Malachy's colleagues in the hospital said to him, 'It's a bloody good job he's gone – he was a ferocious womaniser.' Though his sexual indiscrétions were hushed up in the media, word of mouth was a different thing. A few years later Martin Luther King was shot, and then Robert Kennedy. 'They're killing all the Kennedys,' somebody said, 'I hope Ted gets out of politics.' He didn't, but he had different types of problems after his Chappaquiddick incident, which saw the death of Mary Jo Kopechne, and the barrage of health problems that's always seemed to dog this family.

Malachy's own operating days were nearing an end, however. One day he felt a sore throat coming on and, to avoid infecting his operating team or, more importantly, the patient, he tried to cure it with a medicine called Lincocin. The decision cost him dearly because his system reacted against the medication (which was only recently on the market) and he developed a particularly virulent ulcer which necessitated a stay at the Mayo Clinic in Minnesota.

He drove from Minneapolis to Rochester in the searing heat. It was so humid, birds were literally falling out of the skies along by the Mississippi river. Some of them died; most of them were unable to fly. He was feeling the pressure of the heat himself as well, so much so that he was almost on the point of collapse by the time he reached the clinic. They operated on

The imposing Fort Singleton House, where Dr. Malachy grew up

St. Mary's-on-the-Hill, where he spent four happy years

Portrait of the doctor as a young man

Guy de Chauliac, 1300-1370
Father of Surgery

What the Surgeon Ought to Be

The conditions necessary for the Surgeon are four: First, he should be learned; Second, he should be expert; Third, he must be ingenious, and Fourth, he should be able to adapt himself.

It is required for the First that the Surgeon should know not only the principles of surgery, but also those of medicine in theory and practice; for the Second, that he should have seen others operate; for the Third, that he should be ingenious, of good judgment and memory to recognize conditions; and for the Fourth, that he be adaptable and able to accommodate himself to circumstances.

Let the Surgeon be bold in all sure things, and fearful in dangerous things; let him avoid all faulty treatments and practices. He ought to be gracious to the sick, considerate to his associates, cautious in his prognostications. Let him be modest, dignified, gentle, pitiful, and merciful; not covetous nor an extortionist of money; but rather let his reward be according to his work, to the means of the patient, to the quality of the issue, and to his own dignity.

Ars Chirurgica

This was given to Dr. Malachy after he received his Fellowship

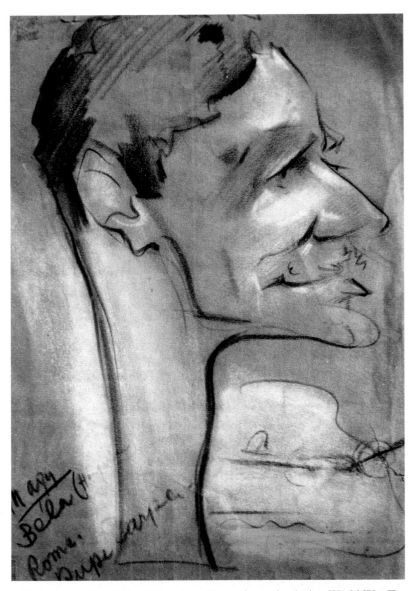

Caricature of the doctor drawn by a Hungarian artist during World War II

The RAF insignia and crest

VF 6796

CERTIFICATE OF SERVICE IN AND DISCHARGE
FROM THE DEFENCE FORCES INCLUDING
SERVICE IN THE VOLUNTEER FORCE.

PART " A."

This is to Certify that No. *115465* Rank *Private*
(Name) *Malachy J. Smyth* born in the
Parish of *Fraugh* in or near the town of
Monaghan in the county of *Monaghan*
was attested at *Dublin* for service in the
Defence Forces on the *8th* day of *June* 1937.
at the age of *23* years and *Two* months;
that from that attestation until the date of this discharge
his service amounts to ———years and ———days
in Army Service and *One* years and *119* days in
Volunteer Service.

This is further to Certify that he was discharged on the
4th day of *October* 1938 for the reasons
hereunder mentioned :—
Resignation
....

(Signature and appointment
of Officer authorising
discharge)
Officer in Charge of Records.

PART " B."

Character during service. (In the handwriting of his
Commanding Officer).
Very Good
U C D Coy Regt of Pass
For Commanding Officer.

Fodhla—Wt. 4665—Gp. 50—6,000—3/'38—P 9896.

Dr. Smyth's certificate of discharge from the Defence Forces

Description of authorised holder as shown on back hereof.

WARNING—If this Certificate of Discharge is lost, a duplicate cannot be issued.

The University of the State of New York

THIS IS TO CERTIFY THAT QUALIFICATIONS FOR PROFESSIONAL
PRACTICE IN NEW YORK STATE HAVING BEEN APPROVED

THE STATE EDUCATION DEPARTMENT

HAS REGISTERED   1287585

SMYTH MALACHY JOSEPH
SLAYTONBUSH LN
UTICA   NY 13501-0000

FOR PRACTICE IN NEW YORK STATE AS A (N)

PHYSICIAN

12/31/91   095593-1
REGISTRATION PERIOD ENDS   LICENSE NO.

COMMISSIONER OF
EDUCATION

SIGNATURE OF REGISTRANT

REGISTRATION CERTIFICATE --- NOT A LICENSE

The doctor's U.S. registration certificate

A painting by Lucy of a racecourse in Saratoga Springs

To all to whom these presents shall come. Greeting

Be it known that by virtue of authority vested in them the Regents of the American College of Surgeons do hereby admit

Malachy J. Smyth

as a

FELLOW

of the College, these letters being their testimonial that he is qualified in the Art and Science of Surgery.

Given at Chicago on the
Fifteenth day of October,
Nineteen Hundred Seventy.

President

Chairman Board of Regents

Secretary

Director

Dr. Smyth's F.A.C.S. certificate

A 'tame' wild duck on Keuka Lake painted by a friend of Lucy

The Medical Society of the State of New York

presents this

Citation

to

Malachy J. Smyth, M.D.

In recognition of Fifty Years devoted to the service
of the public in the practice of medicine.

John H. Carter M.D.
Secretary

Charles Shera Jr. M.D.
President

Citation presented to the doctor by the M.S.S.N.Y. after fifty years

A surgeon using his hands for a different skill

The doctor (right) playing golf in the snow in Utica

BMJ

Can dogs smell
bladder cancer?

Cover of British Medical Journal, 25th September, 2004, Volume 329.

Complete with fez after a sojourn in Cairo

him immediately, at one point even being concerned that his life could have been in danger. (He had ulcerative colitis.) They removed part of his colon and he made a brisk recovery, but he looks back on the whole experience now with wry amusement. 'The doctor who treats himself,' he says. 'has a fool for a patient.'

The second reason he stopped operating was the exorbitant cost of insurance against malpractice. In one year alone this jumped from $2,000 to $50,000, an increase he simply couldn't countenance. 'A man could almost live on $50,000 a year,' he says, 'One would have to be pulling in an incredible revenue to make that outlay practical.' (In today's money, it could be five times that amount).

Not only that, but lawyers were now encouraging patients to have operations for the sole purpose of getting material for lawsuits. The patient was now acting as a kind of *agent provocateur*. In some cases he was doing it so well, the insurance companies couldn't pay up anymore. The doctor was now the remote employee of the legal system, a perverse situation which caused many surgeons to go 'bare', as the expression went. This meant they put all their money into their wives' names. There was no point in suing them because to all intents and purposes they were men of straw. You couldn't get blood out of a stone.

The two events, coupled with some encouragement from Lucy, took him out of operating theatres forever. It was a bittersweet parting but a necessary one. From now on he decided to concentrate totally on his orthopaedic practice and his work with the WCB.

He wasn't the only doctor to cease practising surgery when the astronomical hike took place. In fact there was a mini-evacuation from the ranks in its aftermath. Suddenly everyone was asking questions they never would have in the 'good old days'. Fear of the knife now percolated from patient to surgeon. The latter might not have feared a fatality, but rather the law of the land. It was all getting very ugly and he was relieved to be out of it. This didn't mean he failed to keep in touch with what was happening round about him. Far from it. He watched medical developments with a mixture of awe and apprehension.

Lyndon Johnson became President after Kennedy and escalated the war in Vietnam, contrary to the wishes of the public, especially after the bodybags started coming home, and pictures of atrocities became circulated. Even soldiers became conscientious objectors, burning their draft cards in protest. Suddenly it wasn't the thing to do for GI Joe to follow his leaders on blind faith. America was like the white knight riding over the hill on his charger when Malachy served in World War II but now from a more distant perspective he watched public opprobrium being heaped on it for trying to police the world. 'Hey, hey, LBJ,' the students chorused outside the White House as the flower power era dawned, 'how many kids did you kill today?'

Johnson developed strong Medicare programmes for the elderly and poor but the war decimated his funds and made their continued implementation problematic. As the soldiers' morale dwindled under the increased pressure of Ho Chi Minh and his armies, Johnson finally caved in. He stepped down from the Presidency in 1968 and said he wouldn't run for re-election.

When Nixon ran for the White House again in 1969 he wrote Malachy a letter urging him to vote for him. 'Dear Dr. Smyth,' it went, 'Only a few hours remain before the future of our country will be settled by the polls. We have thus far succeeded, but I can be elected only with your further help. So now, Dr. Smyth, I ask if you will please do this: on Election Day will you persuade at least four of your friends and neighbours in Utica who share our goals to cast their ballots for the ticket.' Ever the manipulator! Some politicians would have been happy to solicit just one vote, but Tricky Dick wanted five. Whatever about his personal integrity, though, his administration was generous to the medical profession in general, and Malachy in particular.

Nixon was elected this time and the year also saw Neil Armstrong land on the moon. The world watched transfixed as he took those first historic steps. Nixon described it as 'the greatest week in the history of the world since the creation'. It had been Kennedy's brainchild but his old nemesis was the man who witnessed it.

Malachy looked on in awe, but many people felt the astronomical expenditure of the space programme was unjustifiable considering problems like hunger in the Third World, which the money could have virtually wiped out. What was the point of looking at a piece of green rock, they pointed out, with some justification, when there were so many problems on our own planet. Malachy wondered what kind of medical research could have been attempted with that kind of money. The evangelist Billy Graham, meanwhile, took issue with Nixon's hyperbole, insisting that there were three greater days than that of the moon landing in history, i.e. those of Christ's birth, death and resurrection. (Nixon, taking the bait, pointed out that he had referred to a week, not three separate days).

Nixon was praised for his foreign policy, particularly with regard to China, but his record on Vietnam was as dismal as that of Johnson. Only when he saw that the war was unwinnable did he withdraw the troops. He declared a ceasefire on January 23, 1974, the very day after Johnson died of a heart attack. There was a grim irony in it all. Shortly afterwards the Watergate scandal blew up, eventually leading to his resignation.

Some commentators pointed out that most presidents eavesdropped in some manner or other on their electoral competitors since the dawn of time but Nixon added insult to injury by his cover-up. In the end it was this that led to his undoing. Now he wasn't just a crook but a liar as well, which most people had suspected anyway.

He never seemed to be able to accept his own failings. 'I gave them a sword and they stuck it in,' was all he could say as he left office, 'Now they won't have Nixon to kick around any more.' Gore Vidal remarked, 'He turned being a crook into a kind of triumph by managing to lose the presidency in a way bigger and more original than anyone else had ever lost it before.'

19

The seventies continued the nomadic pattern of Malachy's life, his work with the WCB taking him all over New York State. Every few weeks he would have to testify about the eligibility of a given patient for disability benefits, which meant upping sticks with Lucy – who doubled as his unofficial secretary – for the duration of the hearing.

His practice was still thriving, thanks in no small measure to the fact that he was ahead of his American counterparts as a result of the more knowledgeable training he had had in England. At times he couldn't cope with the volume of patients in his surgery. The green-eyed monster also raised its ugly head as far as some of his colleagues were concerned. The fact that he was a non-national didn't help either.

One patient he advised on, a famous Quarterback with a prominent American football team, was suffering from a herniated disc. Malachy discussed his predicament with a consultant surgeon. The surgeon decided to perform a laminectomy, which meant a large spinal incision. (A laminectomy consists of removing one of the vertebrae to relieve pressure on the spinal cord). It was major surgery which Malachy didn't agree with, but the consultant forged ahead. The player got short term relief but as time went on the tissues contracted, resulting in even greater pain than he'd had with the disc. His playing career was severely affected, resulting in him moving to a third-rate team. He ended up suing the surgeon for loss of earnings.

'This player was on a $6 million dollar contract a year,' Malachy says, 'which is why I thought putting him under the knife like that was playing with fire. A sportsman's career is relatively short in comparison to other people's. He has to make hay while the sun shines. In this man's case – I won't mention his name because of the litigation involved – brute force wasn't the answer. The laminectomy I performed on the Chief Executive of the Clifton Springs Clinic was different. There was no career risk involved there. The surgeon should have looked beyond the pain to the cause of it. All too often we shoot the messenger – and end up damaging the person it's delivered to as well.'

Another famous person who came into his surgery was a violinist who had a small pain in her finger which made it difficult for her to string her bow. It sounded trivial but had enormous repercussions on her career. He went out to bat for her and secured $30,000 for her in disability benefits. He knew she was *bona fide*, but certain other patients tried to 'swing the lead' so it was important for him to know who he could trust and who was malingering. Sometimes his final decision on the amount of compensation to apply for was down to his gut feeling about a patient's credibility.

He belonged to an exclusive club at this time. Most of the members were doctors. One had to be sponsored by eight people before applying for membership, and then pay a $2,000 bond to the club as well as $200 per month to use its facilities. He played golf here every Thursday and afterwards dined and danced with Lucy in the function room. He would also fraternise with other doctors and swap stories about their respective experiences. One anecdote he heard concerned a man who presented himself at a hospital one day and proceeded to relieve a patient not only of his ready cash but also his car. Only afterwards was it discovered he wasn't a doctor at all.

Malachy was reminded of F.W. Demara, one of the most daring con men of all time who masqueraded not only as a surgeon - at one point even removing a bullet from a patient's heart - but also a dentist, a monk, a psychology lecturer and a prison warden. Tony Curtis played him in the film *The Great Imposter*. 'Demara had more need of a surgical mask than most of us,' Malachy remarks wryly as he reflects upon the imaginative trickster.

There were many exciting medical developments in the seventies. Intensive care facilities improved enormously, as did strides in curing cancer, particularly in children. The first CAT scan machine made its appearance in 1973 and a few years later the first test-tube baby appeared. Towards the end of the decade, the first coronary angioplasty was performed, enabling those with heart problems to avoid more invasive surgery.

Heart transplants were well on the road by this time, Christiaan Barnard having performed the first one in Cape Town in 1967. The heart of the donor came from a 25-year old bank clerk who'd died in a road accident and the recipient was a 53-year-old grocer. He died 18 days after the operation due to tissue rejection but the miracle was that the operation had been performed at all. In subsequent years the ancillary problems would be winnowed out.

Barnard's first operation failed because the drugs used to prevent rejection of the new heart destroyed too much of the patient's natural defence system to fight against infection and he died of double pneumonia. In later operations he leavened the usage of the drugs to allow the body's immune system to kick in on its own, the result being that transplant patients lived for years without problems.

101

In October 1979 the Nobel Prize was won by British scientist Godfrey Hounsfeld for inventing the CAT scan, which enabled pictures of the body to be provided electrically without the invasiveness of an X-ray. Three years later the first artificial heart made its appearance, a 61-year-old dentist by the name of Barney Clark being given a mechanised one made of aluminium and a polyurethane pump in Salt Lake City. The operation was performed by one of the leading lights in the field, William De Vries.

In the early eighties the horrific spectre of AIDS reared its ugly head, but it wasn't until the death of the film star Rock Hudson in 1985 that people really began to sit up and take note. Now the disease had a human, palpable form. Hudson came out of the closet about his homosexuality almost on his deathbed. For many it was too little too late but at least it galvanised people, particularly those in the entertainment field, to campaign vociferously for research into what was generally called 'the gay plague'.

The great researcher Jonas Salk, who had made such wonderful strides in eradicating the virus that produced poliomyelitis by injecting a vaccine into monkeys three decades before, now repeated the same procedure with the HIV virus. The monkeys developed such high levels of HIV antibodies that the virus disappeared. Salk's critics suggested that monkeys were probably naturally resistant to it and that it would have disappeared anyway, thereby rendering his labours fruitless.

AIDS continued its rampage throughout the nineties, as did cancer and heart disease. Early detection was vital, as of course were lifestyle and diet. Unfortunately, the U.S. was very much a sedentary society and was turning into a couch potato one, which meant that obesity was now becoming an increasingly serious problem. Keep fit regimens worked in tandem with this, coupled with a plethora of diet books which seemed to polarise the country. Many of its residents seemed to make it their ambition to reach anorexic status, while the rest looked like they wanted to eat their way into oblivion. Drug addiction also seemed to take an exponential leap, and of course was as instrumental as sex in the steady rise in death rates from AIDS.

Malachy continued to wear his two hats of doctor and legal advisor as he travelled to various locales throughout New York with Lucy to adjudicate on disability hearings. Then it was back to the daily grind of his consultancy rooms, with the occasional foray to the Finger Lakes to recharge his batteries. Here he would entertain on his boat and enjoy the plethora of animals that proliferated: squirrels, deer, chickadees, wild turkeys, black bears and even snakes. Wild ducks would also parade onto his deck frequently, looking anything but wild as they pranced about, oblivious to everything but the little flock of ducklings that brought up the rear. Sometimes they sat preening themselves beside himself and his friends on land, undeterred even by barking dogs. They simply enjoyed company.

He also owned three-quarters of an acre of land in Florida near Fort Myer and often golfed down there. This was a 'back to nature' exercise as alligators from the nearby swamps frequently invaded the golf course. One day his ball landed on the back of an alligator that was sleeping on the course close to the pin. As Malachy approached, he got up and walked towards the hole, dropping the ball as he did so. An argument subsequently erupted among the players as to whether he was allowed to play from where the friendly alligator dropped it, anxious as he was to improve Malachy's handicap! (Maybe this reptile could have enabled him to secure a birdie, if that isn't mixing up one's zoology too much.)

Another day himself and his fellow players were waiting to drive off when they saw a man ahead of them taking an inordinate amount of time to get out of a bunker. When they eventually decided to have a word with him they saw he had actually passed out. They carried him back to the clubhouse but it was too late: he had suffered a massive coronary. (Some people might say it was the happiest way one could pick to die.)

Bing Crosby also died on a golf course, his alleged last words being 'That was a great game, fellers.' Malachy heard of another man on his own course who dropped dead after teeing off at the 12th hole. The players at the hole behind him on the day weren't as perturbed by his untimely passing as the fact that (a) play was severely disrupted by his demise, and (b) the ambulance driver damaged the course when he drove across the grass to examine him. A meeting was held the following day to try and find a way to keep old fogies with dodgy tickers off the precious fairways! One is reminded of Bill Shankly's famous dictum: 'Football isn't a matter of life and death – it's much more important than that.' Maybe the Florida golf course should have had a notice in the clubhouse saying: 'Members Are Advised Not To Die Before They Have Completed A Round To Avoid Inconvenience To Those On The Tee Behind Them. Mild Coronaries Are Also To Be Avoided, Except In Outlying Bunkers'. (A more succinct one could go: 'Strokes Interfere With Strokes').

Malachy was greatly saddened to hear of the riding accident of the actor Christopher Reeve in 1995. Reeve had played Superman in the film of that name and, like many previous stars who had donned the cape of the comic strip hero, succumbed to what eventually came to be called 'the Superman curse'. Reeve took what appeared to be a simple fall from his horse, who refused a jump, and was paralysed from the neck down as a result. At the age of 42 he had to face the fact that he was, to all intents and purposes, an infant with little or no control over his bodily functions. Activities which the rest of us take for granted, like having a cup of tea or going to the toilet, became almost like military activities involving a large number of people. He couldn't be left alone for even a minute for fear of undergoing potentially fatal breathing difficulties.

Reeve was an athletic man so his enforced immobility hit him harder than it would have had most people. He became a veritable vegetable, a prisoner inside his own body. His mind was hyperactive and this worsened his predicament. He tried to will himself better, which made some disabled societies leery of him. He was accused of being an enemy of disabled people by insisting that one day he would walk again. He was the wrong kind of role model for them, the thinking went.

'Why me?' he asked himself, 'Why didn't I put my hands out and break my fall?' He was never overly religious, but now a strong negativity vibe set in. If there was a God, he concluded, He wasn't benevolent – he was malign. God caused the tragedy.

One of the last films Reeve made before his accident featured him playing a paraplegic. To research it, he went into a hospital to see the disabled at first hand. He learned how to move like a wheelchair victim, unaware he would soon become one for real. In a few short months, there would be no director to shout 'Cut' as he got out of his chair to resume normal services.

'Until Memorial Day 1995,' Reeve once said, 'my body had never let me down. I thought I was indestructible.' That was the day Superman fell to earth with a vengeance. Not only could Clark Kent not fly, he couldn't even walk. 'When two people have to roll you back and forth in order to put on your underpants at the age of 45,' he mused, 'it's a difficult lesson in patience and acceptance.' Such people literally held his life in their hands.

A particular area of interest to Reeve – and Malachy – was research to do with growing nerves across gaps in the spinal cords of rats. Such cords were severed by researchers, but after a cell transportation across a gap of no more than one-fifth of an inch, the rats started to flex their hind legs. A year later they were able to support their own weight and move their legs more actively. The downside was that the nerves that were grafted onto the rats' spinal cords were from the peripheral nervous system, which regenerates, unlike the central nervous system in humans, which doesn't. Reeve's wry reaction to this news was, 'Oh to be a rat.'

His humour kept him sane, right up until his untimely death in 2004. Perhaps this wasn't surprising considering one of his best friends was a colleague from acting school, Robin Williams. Whenever Williams called to Reeve's house, Reeve would greet him with the comment, 'You'll forgive me if I stay seated.' He'd learned to laugh through his tears.

He was initially tempted to end his life but instead of that turned his problem around by becoming a spokesman for people suffering from spinal injuries throughout the U.S., most of whom hadn't his financial comforts. He raised hundreds of thousands of dollars through the Christopher Reeve Foundation, most of which went to the American Paralysis Association. He also lobbied politicians to finance research into spinal cord injuries.

Bill Clinton listened to him and in 1998 increased NIH funding by over $1 billion, with a promise that such an increase would be repeated every year for the next five years. The best way to save money in the long run, Reeve advised, was in the area of prevention rather than treatment. Over $5 billion a year, he pointed out, was spent on merely keeping people with spinal cord injuries 'ticking'. If even $40 million of that was spent on research, he contended, it would make better sense than trying to repair the hole in the spinal cord bucket, as it were, and also hopefully wage war on other diseases like multiple sclerosis, Parkinsons and Alzheimer's.

As far as Malachy's own research went he hadn't got many more answers to the conundrums posed by lumbar pain but he was still as excited as ever by the challenge. Maybe, he thought, the real the thrill was in the search rather than the solution.

Not that the latter was ever likely. Just as each age brought cures to the diseases of yesteryear, so also did it bring new diseases. And so the circle turned. Doctors put medicines of which they knew little into bodies of which they knew less and some of their patients thrived on them and some didn't. Everyone was on a learning curve and the man in the clouds laughed heartily every time an innovator whooped in joy. Because He knew the cure, in some ways, was always going to be worse than the disease. Or at least to have side-effects that would cause even more headaches to the supposed beneficiaries of it.

Still, all you could do was put your head down and take one day, and one patient, at a time. There may have been no guarantees with any form of treatment but the more miles you had on the clock the better you got at knowing which ones to apply. That was one advantage human beings had over cars – perhaps the only one.

20

Like most physicians, Malachy often travelled to medical conventions. Nearly twenty years after the publication of his groundbreaking article 'Sciatica and the Intervertebral Disc' a peculiar thing happened to him at one of them.

The American Academy of Orthopaedic Surgeons was having its fall meeting in Miami, and many of the leading researchers in the country were slated to be there. As well as those from the U.S. and Canada, there were also going to be luminaries from Japan, India, South Africa and Europe. In fact the whole spectrum of orthopaedics was going to be touched upon one way or the other. Apart from the large series of papers being read, one could meet the surgeons privately and glean a little more inside information. It would also be a great social occasion. There would also be a banquet and a ball.

He had to be there. He had letters from all the major world orthopaedic centres. He was greatly looking forward to exchanging ideas with some of the people from these places.

The day finally arrived and Lucy and himself made their way to the American Hotel in Florida, their hearts fluttering.

That evening he went through the usual formalities of registration, signing his name and getting a tag to pin onto his coat. He also indicated that he would be taking part in some of the tours. He would most certainly be at the banquet.

He'd taken note of the fact that a major part of the meeting was being devoted to pain, particularly pain associated with a herniated disc. He was rather smug about this. After all, he *owned* that kind of pain! (He was just lending it to the symposium organisers for the purpose of discussion.)

The next morning he sat in the great lecture-hall in the semi-darkness listening to the papers being read from the rostrum. He wasn't sure at first, but a name kept being mentioned which sounded like Smith. He concentrated more closely to catch it again. This time it was pronounced 'Smythe'. It didn't occur to him that it was himself they were talking about.

The penny dropped a few minutes later when one of his original drawings showing pain passing down the leg was shown. He recognised it instantly as his own. He was surprised that the organisers hadn't invited him to sit on the panel at the end of the readings to answer questions. And yet in a way he was glad they didn't. He was just as happy to remain anonymous. However, he did go down to the four man panel and moderator of the meeting to introduce himself, as a matter of courtesy.

'Hello,' he said to no one in particular, 'I'm the Dr. Smyth you've been quoting all evening.' Everyone looked blankly at him as if he was the perpetrator of a rather silly prank. Finally, one of the inscrutable gentlemen behind the table said, 'Hi. We weren't sure you'd be able to make it.' Malachy detected a note of irony in the way he said this. It was as if he was part of a prank too. He felt a sinking feeling in his gut.

The moderator was called over and Malachy approached him.

'I'm Malachy Smyth,' he said again.

'Really?' the moderator replied, 'That's interesting, because Dr Smyth died a few years ago.'

'Well if he did,' Malachy shot back, 'He's just been resurrected.'

He felt somewhat surreal hearing his own obituary delivered like this. All he could do was fight fire with fire.

He was reminded of *Hamlet* without the prince. Unfortunately, he was being cast more in the role of Banquo's ghost in *Macbeth*.

The moderator came forward and addressed him somewhat sternly.

'I'm afraid I don't know who you are,' he snorted, 'but my records show that Dr. Smyth passed away a few years ago. I refer to the Dr. Smyth whose research work has recently been published as a classic in *Clinical Orthopaedics and Related Research*.'

'Thank you,' Malachy replied, 'To tell you the truth, I was rather pleased with it myself.'

Again the moderator gave him a funny look. Maybe he was thinking about calling security to remove this strange man who was claiming to be the medical world's answer to Lazarus.

Was this all he had to show for his years burning the midnight oil as he surveyed endless arrays of X-rays and medical reports – to be mistaken for an impostor at his own symposium? Was the medical profession going to be reduced to researchers leapfrogging over one another to be first in the queue with some new revelation or insight? Nobody needed to tell him that the work mattered more than the man who put his name to it, but when the wrong name had been appended, something needed to be done.

He wasn't greedy for glory but if somebody else was, and was willing to use devious means to attain it, it was time to stop him in his tracks. There was too much competition in the profession already. It was like the old joke about the two consultants arguing over the patient on the operating table and one saying dispassionately to the other, 'Wait till you see – the autopsy will prove I'm right.'

It was obvious to him that he'd been deemed to be an impostor. If so, he wouldn't have been the first person to try this. He was well aware of people in the past who had wormed their way into these kinds of conferences for mischief. In fact he and Lucy had met one such soul themselves at a recent dinner for orthopaedic surgeons. She was a flamboyant lady who crashed her way into a banquet and talked ninety to the dozen until the waiter came round looking for her ticket and she didn't have one. This lady had class. She stalked off in high dudgeon at the 'discourtesy' shown to her.

He didn't wish to suffer a similar fate. That afternoon he skipped the meetings and took himself down to the medical library at Miami University. The librarian promptly got him the edition of *Clinical Orthopaedics* that he wanted. He leafed through the book and found what he was looking for.

In the introductory pages he spotted his article, labelled 'The Classic.' On each side of the top of the page was a photograph. The one on the right was that of his friend and co-author. The one on the left bore the inscription M. J. Smyth. But the man in the picture was most assuredly not himself. To add to the confusion, the caption also indicated that he had died. Slowly but surely, the facts of the matter started to dawn on him. He phoned the editor of the journal and explained his predicament. 'Rumours of my death,' he remarked *a la* Mark Twain, 'have been greatly exaggerated.'

It turned out that that other man, a Michael Joseph Smyth (Malachy's initials were also M.J.) had died in 1964. How obvious the error seemed now.

The matter was cleared up a few weeks later. Dr. Malachy Smyth was alive again, the editor having explained that the man assigned to gather all the facts about his work was in fact the man who was really dead.

Before this assistant passed away, he found an M.J. Smyth, but got no further. He didn't manage to trace Malachy.

So there were two M.J. Smyths on the planet. But the other one had never written a medical article. If the editor had waited and cross-checked his facts he wouldn't have made the crucial error.

'I don't know if the other M.J. Smyth ever found out he had been credited with writing a classic article on the intervertebral disc,' Malachy says today, 'If he did, he kept very quiet about it. Maybe he relished the publicity surrounding it. But there was no way he could have passed himself off as me in front of so many people at the conference, especially since I was there myself.' He then adds wryly, 'I'm also better-looking than he was!'

Sadly, the error meant he was prevented from addressing an audience of a thousand people about his work. His practice was also damaged for a while afterwards. He's still intrigued as to how the other man's photograph could have appeared without his permission but he doesn't lose any sleep over the issue. 'It could have been much worse,' he laughs, 'I could have died instead of him. The main thing was that I was alive.'

And he still is. Very much alive, actually. In fact more so than many men half his age, as anyone who meets him will realise immediately. Curiosity, and the passion to help those less well off than himself, has given him the elixir of eternal youth. On the cusp of his ninetieth year he's prospering well on it. Maybe, he thinks, there's something in this medical lark after all.

21

Towards the end of their time in the U.S., Lucy suffered a stroke. She recovered physically but was in poor spirits a lot of the time. Malachy felt she'd have a better quality of life in Ireland. She agreed, so they decided to come back to Sligo. They returned to Rosses Point, the place where Christy O'Connor had taught her to golf all those years ago. She was past her golfing days now, sadly, and it pained him to watch the vivacity disappearing from her. He became her doctor as well as her husband for the remainder of her life.

Going home on the plane was almost a surreal experience, the jumbled memories of the past merging in his head like the spools of an old movie he played over and over, freeze-framing the seminal moments like skeletons that tried to escape from him but couldn't.

The corpse of Pastor Carhalton, and the ivy clawing at it like a human thing. The ghosts of the British troops round what Patrick Kavanagh called the 'uncurious' hills of Shancoduff. The wrench of leaving his parents and family to live in the Big Smoke. The years of grinding study, lit up only by shafts of hope, like your rugby team scoring a winning try in the last minute. Meeting somebody like Ned Wilcox who refused to toe the line. Wondering how much older his parents would look the next time he saw them. Delivering his first baby and realising how simple it all was, as if nobody needed a doctor really, because all he was was a witness to the age-old miracle of life.

Graduation, and the never-ending search for the root of pain, which eluded him like a fox in a covert. The Blitz in Devon with every building a ticking bomb, the tension dissipated by ludicrous incidents like the man who tried to run away from his operating table. Being brought back to the dread of it all the night his friend Max left a cigarette butt shimmering in an ash-tray and never came back to finish it, too busy dying for his country. So much suffering, so many mysteries – and each age finding a new way to kill us. No wonder Kavanagh spoke of World War II as 'that bit of Munich bother.' Maybe that comment typified the tunnel vision of every small area in Ireland, every small area in the world. All politics, as the man said, was local.

He would never forget that cigarette butt, nor would he ever forget the

Middle East, where the deposed troops of a demented Field Marshal looked forlornly for their head and found only the banality of civilian tasks in a strange country. But life wasn't about how much punishment you could mete out, it was about what you did when you couldn't mete it out anymore.

He witnessed a different kind of pain in Leeds, where the fugitive faces of those looking for the Last Chance Saloon turned up every day. Then there was the ballerina who'd lost her rhythm; the woman in the car accident with her scalp pulled down over her face; the compensation fraudster who dropped his crutches as a car raced towards him; the man who couldn't feel pain; the woman who failed to believe she was cured; the terminal cancer patient who was treated as nothing but … a terminal cancer patient.

These were the tools of his trade, the problems without which he would have no relevance, the thorny enigmas that kept him awake at nights, the jigsaws missing a piece. The missing piece of his own personal jigsaw was found when he met Lucy, the woman who persuaded him not be too impetuous, who taught him that a doctor who had no patience would have no patients – the lesson Ned Wilcox learned all those years ago. After he met her he learned to put things in perspective, learned that the world wasn't going to end tomorrow. She was his anchor and his lamp, a simple girl who brought out the simplicity in himself in whatever corner of the globe they inhabited.

Paris, Florence, Bologna. The day she sat in a royal chair in the Louvre and got ticked off. Drinking with him in Napoleon's chateau. Haggling with the boulevardiers of the Champs Elysses, or giggling at the ladies of easy virtue as they made their way home. Years later going to the Smithsonian Institute with her, or the Army and Navy Museum to check out details of his ancestors who were part of the 1849 Gold Rush. The day she hurt her knee and wasn't able to bring up the gifts at Mass at the church of the Immaculate Conception, everyone merely thinking she was shy. Listening to him endlessly as he made plans for his great medical breakthrough. Comforting him whenever he got thwarted in his aims, the way every man gets thwarted and every woman has sense enough to know it will happen and not nag him about it.

Travelling round with him afterwards as he locked horns with the authorities in their field, bewildered sometimes by the manner in which he had these people on such pedestals, seeing them all as just other searchers for the holy grail, as if all medical people were equal in this passionate quest; even if some of them were celebrities and some just foot-soldiers fanning the flame.

He picked the brains of these men in an effort to emulate them, only to realise that he was going in a different direction than they were. He still looked up to them as time went on, but from a different angle now, because he'd found his own voice, his own mantra. It wasn't like a road to Damascus or a re-inventing of the wheel, but the day he realised he could turn pain on and off like a tap something clicked inside his head and stayed there.

He listened to this mantra every time he heard a patient complain of an ache or pain, every time his scalpel bit into their flesh, every time he thought he saw a solution to an old conundrum that wasn't just a mirage. He felt the excitement of a child when he cured people, but not everybody could be cured. And then one day it was over, the lawyers and opportunists edging him into a desk job, exchanging his surgical robes for a pinstripe suit and a pencil as he fought a different kind of war from the sidelines.

Himself and Lucy made a new life for themselves in Ireland. Her father had left her some land in Rosses Point, a seafaring village in Sligo, and it was to here they returned. W.B. Yeats spent his childhood years here, swimming the beaches and climbing the cliffs with his brother Jack, the painter, and both of them wrote about this in their later years. Their house was just a stone's throw from the golf course, which is famous worldwide. Rumour has it that Yeats found the view from the elevated third tee to be one of the most astounding in the country. The par four second hole also offers a sensational view from the green. The next stop is New York! (But no, it isn't true that you can see Utica on a fine day from here.)

They arrived back in Rosses Point just before the course celebrated its centenary in 1994, the year Padraig Harrington won the Irish Amateur Championship there. Jutting into Drumcliff Bay at the end of a small peninsula just four miles north of Sligo town, it was designed by George Coombe, the founding secretary of the Golfing Union of Ireland, but revamped in 1927. It was then enlarged from 9 to 18 holes. At one point it was regarded as the 14th best course in the world and many legends played on it, including Bobby Locke, Nick Faldo, Walter Hagen and Tom Watson. (Watson regards the 14th hole – nominally a par 4 but effectively a par 5 when a treacherous wind is blowing in from the sea – as one of the most challenging he's ever played on.) It has hosted the West of Ireland Amateur Championship since 1923.

Apart from golf, Rosses Point is well known for its mussels, its mackerel and pollock and of course its salmon. Austie's pub is a much-loved hostelry and the Yeats County Hotel a popular place to stay while sight-seeing.

The land Lucy had been bequeathed was on the banks of the Garavogue river. There was a coastguard station on it which had been built by the British at the time of the Armada to keep the Spaniards from coming ashore. It was now in ruins but its base was very strong. The IRA had attempted to blow it up but only partially succeeded. (Lord Louis Mountbatten, the Queen's cousin, was also assassinated by the IRA some years later in Mullachmore when they exploded a remote-controlled 50lb bomb on his boat Shadow V. Mountbatten was Commander-In-Chief for the Royal Navy in South East Asia during World War II and later Viceroy of India during the transfer of power from Britain to that country.)

Malachy asked a local man who had recently bought some powerful equipment to demolish it for him. The man pushed the whole fortress into the sea. It was like a symbolic act, removing the last British structure from the Republic.

Soon afterwards he built a house on the land. The end of the lawn sloped down to the shores of the river, which reached the sea only a mile away. He built a curved series of steps which went all the way down to his private dock area. Boats could now anchor here at high tide. Salmon also swam by on their way to spawn in Lough Gill. In fact the first salmon to be caught in Ireland was said to have breathed its last in these waters. (It was given to the local bishop in accordance with tradition.)

The retired Dr Smyth now received a pleasant surprise because it turned out that fishermen from all over the world wanted to come and fish from his dock. He was informed he could charge them up to £2,000 per year to avail of his choice location so this he did. The first 'rods' (as they were called) were from Argentina, and they were soon followed by many others. In no time at all he realised that he had something of a goldmine at the bottom of his garden. Who needed medicine! This was much less stressful.

He also became very interested in the Atlantic Salmon Trust, a UK organisation which champions wild salmon and sea trout, working for their conservation as well as conducting marine and freshwater research. It's an independent charity which receives no Government funding. It's based in Perthshire and gratefully welcomes all patrons.

One of Malachy's neighbours was Kathleen O'Hara, who had been married to Lucy's brother Frank. Frank sadly passed away twenty years ago but Kathleen is still hale and hearty. A piano teacher by trade, she also plays the organ in church. She speaks admiringly of Dr Malachy. 'No matter what life has thrown at him he always seems to bounce back,' she says. 'I envy him his nature. He seems to be able to put all the ups and downs in a box and move on.'

Kathleen is one of a family of eight. Five of her six brothers were sea captains so she has this in her blood. She also boasts the best view in Rosses Point from her back garden, where she can see Oyster Island, Coney Ireland and Knocknarea, the mountain Yeats often wrote about. The wind still bundles up the clouds here, giving the sky an ominous look as they hover over the hinterland.

Kathleen, daughter of the former Rosses Point harbourmaster, was glad to be able to get to know the returned emigrants better in Rosses Point, not having had the opportunity to do so during their globetrotting years. They also struck up an acquaintance with Father Dolan, the resident monsignor, and the local police sergeant John Conlon, of whom they were equally fond. The closely-knit community of the Connacht bolthole was doubly inviting to them after all of their time in relative anonymity in the U.S.

At present Dr Malachy is conversing with Kathleen about the possibility of using the dock area at the back of her own property for interested fishermen. As of yet this is all 'pie in the sky' as far as Kathleen is concerned. Neither would she be overly enthused about the invasion of her privacy it would entail.

When I ask her what her abiding memory of Malachy would be, she says, 'His excitability when he was gardening. He was out in all weathers buying shrubs in the local nursery or cataloguing his trees. Gardening was wonderful therapy for both of them.'

They spent six happy years here, even if Lucy wasn't the woman she had once been. Malachy fished and played golf when he wasn't gardening and she sometimes joined him on the course to watch, or perhaps read a book nearby. She also organised many horse shows as medical fundraisers. It was a mellow period of their lives with time almost appearing to stand still. Lucy also continued to paint, as contented with herself in the beauty of her surroundings as she had once been in Utica.

But as the century neared its close she suffered another stroke and was more severely debilitated this time, her congenital heart defect coming against her. Malachy didn't expect her to recover from this and she didn't. And then she died, and he had to figure out what to do without her.

Memories of her came to him unbidden at every turn and indulging them had its price. Every landmark reminded him of her, every blade of grass and swerve of shore. He knew he couldn't live in Rosses Point anymore so he decided to go back to Monaghan.

It was another wrench, but a necessary one. He was continuing his nomadic existence but this was his first solitary journey in countless years. He hadn't been without her since after the war. It was almost as if his shadow had disappeared. Or a limb. This was a different kind of amputation, a different kind of referred pain.

Religion became a poultice to put over the raw wound of her absence. He became comforted by the thought that they'd meet again. 'Don't know where, don't know when', as the song said, but sometime.

He believes there's a divinity that shapes our ends. Some things have to be accepted on blind faith.

'She was a strong woman and she'd want me to be strong,' he says, 'that's the best way to honour her.' To that end he doesn't dwell on her passing because he knows she wouldn't have wanted that. They had a charmed life together and he has many treasured memories of that to carry him through. She was his solid support through a topsy-turvy life but now he has to do it on his own.

The older he gets, the more he finds himself looking back on the early years of his life, the time he spent in Fort Singleton House, his home in Monaghan, and later in Mespil Road after his parents moved to Dublin. He didn't spend as much time with them as he would have liked because of the constraints of his job, which gives rise to a mixture of wistfulness and regret. 'Fort Singleton House is a hotel now, ' he says. 'I went back there a few years ago but the atmosphere wasn't good. The people running it didn't welcome me or my family. It cured any sentiment I might otherwise have had.' The house in Dublin was a happier one (his mother in particular loved the city) for all concerned. He looks back with fondness on simple things like trips to Haddington Road church and a meal afterwards: the little routines that are all of our lives.

He still gets excited about rugby games, and also loves books. Hillary Clinton's autobiography is the last one he read. (He appears to be more interested in her than in her husband.)

At the moment he's reading the memoirs of Maureen O'Hara, *Tis Herself*. This actress was actually a distant relative of Lucy (whose maiden name, of course, was O'Hara). 'She resembles her in temperament too,' Malachy says, 'fiery and stubborn – but fiercely loyal.'

One time when the pair of them were staying in the Roosevelt Hotel on Hollywood Boulevard they saw the flame-haired beauty's name encased in glass on the pavement outside. It was one of a thousand such cases embedded into the cement, each in the shape of a star and filled with crushed crimson stone. This was as close at they got to seeing a celebrity. They were there to attend an orthopaedic conference – what else. Dr Malachy has always been more drawn to operating theatres than actors' ones.

He also likes to read books about athletes with medical problems. The healing of sporting injuries remains his prime concern. It bothers him deeply to think of players throwing their careers down the drain as a result of getting inappropriate treatment for their problems. His own rugby-playing career was cut short by injury so he feels an added empathy for these people. He keeps coming back to the Quarterback who had the laminectomy, or those who have surgery too hastily.

Another memory that keeps springing to mind is the time he could have died from colitis, when he went to the Mayo Clinic. Also the huge rise in medical insurance that precipitated his move away from surgery and into the Workers' Compensation Board. He remembers standing in the WCB office one day on a floor so high up in the Twin Towers that he was actually looking downwards on the planes flying outside. Who could have known that thirty years down the road so many hundreds of people would look out at a similar scene ... except this time a plane would actually have crashed into the floor below them. What thoughts would have flooded through their minds as they first suspected an accident, and then terrorism, and then became gripped by panic as they realised there was no way out for them except to jump? It was too tortuous to contemplate.

He keeps his mind off the past by constant activity. He played a huge part in the writing of this book, rising to the challenge of dredging his memory banks with great enthusiasm, quoting his near-namesake Betty Smith's apothegm, 'Writing a book is like having a baby: its conception is more fun than its completion.'

He displayed similar wit when speaking of his second cousin James F. Smith, who served under General MacArthur's father in the Spanish-American war in the Philippines. Jim became a Brigadier-General and took an active part in the campaign both before and after the surrender of Manila. He was then appointed Collector of Customs, one of the most important posts in the Civil Administration, and finally to the Supreme Court. He was conceived in Monaghan and crossed the Atlantic in an intra-uterine manner. Malachy jokes, 'He always liked to travel in comfort'. He was finally born after a very rough crossing. Malachy stayed with his sister for a time when he was in Monterey; she was 90 then.

'Don't worry too much about strict chronology,' he advised as we tried to join the dots of his picaresque life, 'I'd like this to be a book of sensations rather than a diary. There's very little to say about some years of my life, and too much to say about others.' Maybe it's the same for all of us. The devil – and angel – is in the detail.

The past is a distant country. Memories have to be jogged, long-distant ones mixing with the more immediate in a quixotic melange. It's a long way from Monaghan to the Middle East but he's been there, done that. Home now, the salmon swimming upstream to where he was spawned, he has the time to sift through the patchwork quilt of experience to try and find out what it all meant, all the enigmatic mysteries, all the wild searches. Some of the years seem like a blur while others are crystal clear, and they seem to have slipped by almost without him noticing. It's as if somebody flicked their finger and he was in a time machine. In many ways he's still the young man who wanted to change the world, who wanted to 'kill' pain.

Though he's out of the medical firing-line, he makes it his business to keep himself in touch with all of the latest developments by reading magazines like the *British Medical Journal* (to which he's a subscriber) and the *British Journal of Sports Medicine*. One that intrigues him particularly is the fact that dogs are now being used to diagnose bladder cancer. This form of cancer creates an odour in one's urine which only dogs, with their superior sense of smell, can detect. He's both amused and impressed by this phenomenon. 'Who says you can't teach an old dog new tricks?' he asks.

The possibility that canines might be able to detect malignant tumours on the basis of odour was first put forward in a letter to *The Lancet* in 1989, which was inspired by a doctor's consultation with a woman who claimed to have sought medical help as a result of her dog's inordinate interest in a skin lesion, which subsequently proved to be a malignant melanoma. A number of researchers subsequently decided to investigate the possibility of dogs being used to detect odours in the urinary tract that hinted at 'rogue' causes.

Gillian Lacey, the lady in question, got together with a group of scientists who spearheaded the research. Her problem, she said, was that hospitals couldn't give her a lump of cancer the same way they might be able to provide a lump of sugar as a reward.

Six dogs of varying breeds and ages completed a seven month period of training. They were first required to differentiate between the odour of urine in healthy people and unhealthy ones and then, narrowing the focus, to distinguish between those who were unhealthy because of bladder cancer or as a result of some other condition such as cystitis or benign prostatic hyperplasia.

Some of the dogs hit a stumbling block here. They were confused by the fact that they had been rewarded for pouncing upon unhealthy urine and were now being asked to ignore this because it wasn't unhealthy in the appropriate way. It was a lot to ask and it was here, perhaps expectably, that their success rate dropped from 90% to 41%. However, considering traditional methods of urine analysis only yielded a success rate of 14%, it was a dramatic improvement.

Sniffer dogs, of course, have for a long time been used to detect drugs at airports and prisons and so on, and also to track down escaped convicts or suspected criminals by being given an item of their clothing to smell. It's well-known that dogs are fascinated by urine. Observe one at a lamp-post if you're in any doubt. But not until now has this predilection been exploited for medical benefits.

Throughout history animals have been used as guinea pigs, but all too rarely has their sensory sensitivity been exploited for maximum effect. We know that dogs can hear high-pitched sounds that humans can't. Ditto for mice. This is why ultra-sound devices are often used to get rid of household mice. During World War I, parrots, whose sense of hearing is also acute, were kept on top of the Eiffel Tower to warn soldiers of enemy aircraft, being able to detect planes long before they came into the range of the human look-out towers.

An acute sense of hearing, unfortunately, can't be of much medical benefit, but an acute sense of smell can. Gillian Lacey's experiment could pave the way for further research into other diseases. Maybe insects could even be used. It's a well known fact that the male gypsy moth, to name but one, can smell the female from nearly two miles away.

'Wouldn't it be great if dogs could smell herniated discs?' he suggests. 'Everyone could have their own personal Fido to save them a trip to the doctor.' (The downside would be that doctors would undergo a dramatic reduction in their revenue.)

He also remembers goats being used as guinea pigs for hip replacement when he worked in England. 'They weren't reluctant patients,' he says. 'They jumped up on the table and put their leg out as if they were looking forward to the anaesthetic. After a few weeks they were gambolling round the fields as if nothing happened.'

These are optimistic thoughts, but sometimes one feels that while researchers are fixated on dreams of the future, the sad present laughs at it. By which I mean that the health services in this country are in a state of near-permanent chaos. Any money the government throws at them, according to various ministers, disappears into a black hole.

There are interminable queues at A&E units. People are dying in the streets because of being in equally never-ending queues for heart operations. Patients spend days on hospital trolleys because of the notorious bed shortage. Many people also find themselves in A&E units simply because they can't afford to go to their GP.

The interns in these units are worked off their feet. Many of them end up emigrating to greener pastures. So also do many nurses, especially those studying for Intensive Care qualifications. The result could be that we have a dearth of Irish people in medicine. This is happening in the clerical world too. Vocations are at an all-time low, which means that in the next generation we could be preached to by the 'black babies' of Africa which we once contributed to in order to rescue them from Godlessness. A mix of both would be ideal.

The lifestyle of the average 'Celtic Tiger' resident has also led to unforeseen problems. Executive stress is steadily moving up the food chain as a killer. Needless to say, the Irish also drink too much. We've always done so, but it's getting worse. Women and children are now joining the ranks of the infamous binge culture. Then there's the epidemic of teenage suicides, particularly among males, and the ubiquitous HIV virus, not to mention the increase in other sexually-transmitted diseases.

Diet is another bugbear. Our ancestors may have regarded spaghetti bolognese as an exotic dish, but now with nouvelle cuisine and dining al fresco and whatnot we've become quite trendy. Or at least some of us have. As with everything else, Ireland is a two-tiered society today. Many of us suffer from obesity while others, nurtured on the stick insect image of magazine covers, descend into anorexia nervosa and bulimia. Such extremes seem to typify our attitude to everything else as well. We worship our bodies and yet we don't seem to respect them. The contradiction may be exemplified by such practices as burning ourselves up with machines that give us fake tans and then getting pasty from lack of fresh air.

Prosperity comes at a price, and so does liberalism. Ireland today is making the same mistakes England did a decade ago, and America a decade before that. We've built more and more gyms because of our sedentary lifestyle, but it all seems to be something of a vicious circle. We drive to the letterbox to post a letter because we're too lazy to walk, and then spend fifteen minutes on the treadmill to ease our conscience. We eat organic foods and then smoke our way to lung cancer. We have seaweed baths at exorbitant expense to unwind, and then die prematurely of executive stress. We pay exorbitant rates at health farms to compensate for our fast food lifestyle. We've made old age sexy, but not enough of us reach it.

Malachy doesn't get too depressed about these phenomena, preferring to dwell on the number of positives about the modern world. 'When I started out,' he says, 'there was no cure for TB, no cure for polio, no hip replacements, no antibiotics. People could be forced to stay in bed permanently if they broke their hips. Before the end of World War II, fatalities resulting from conditions like diphtheria and whooping cough were almost inevitable. Neither were there any drugs for rheumatoid arthritis or schizophrenia.'

We were still a long way away from open heart surgery, test tube babies and transplantation of organs. A cancer diagnosis was also commonly regarded as a death sentence. 'We have to realise how far we've come. When I was working in hospitals during the war, the conditions were often Dickensian. Death was round every corner. Intensive care was still a distant concept, so people were wheeled straight from operating theatres back to their wards, which left them susceptible to every kind of infection you could mention. The hygiene was rudimentary also, but what could you do? There was a war going on. These wards were often like chambers of horrors. There was also a lot of ignorance around. The connection between cigarettes and cancer hadn't even been properly established.' To this extent, he applauds the smoking ban in public places today – including, of course, pubs.

As regards where medicine goes from here, he has a special interest in researchers finding out what kind of electricity comes from a nerve end. If we could discover this, he contends, we could possibly re-start electrical continuity and cure paralysis.

He believes there may well be many chemicals involved in causing pain. He also thinks that it might eventually be possible to use a specific chemical to produce a specific pain. 'The way the situation stands at present,' he complains, 'is the blunderbuss approach – hit everything with an analgesic and one is bound to get a quick fix result.'

Such a mindset seems to suit today's executive generation who want the ten second cure – because everything else seems to take just ten seconds. Deferred gratification doesn't seem to come into the picture. They just want Dr Feelgood. Now – or even sooner.

He denigrates the 'pill for every ill' culture, the carpet bomb technique of drug prescriptions which overlook root causes. He's particularly perturbed about what he perceives to be the mistreatment of athletes suffering from tendonitis and suchlike. All too often they're pumped up with cortisone injections which have the comforting effect of reducing inflammation and swelling, and also improving the movement of structures round the joints but which, in his view, could do long term damage to their tissues and result in their careers being cut short.

Cortisone was regarded almost as a 'miracle' drug when it first came on the scene, having the advantage over antibiotics that it mobilised the body's capacity to heal itself. But like every miracle drug it came with a price tag. All too often it was regarded as a cure-all, a panacea for any undiagnosed or undiagnosable condition. This scattergun approach – 'We don't know what he's suffering from, so give him some cortisone' – was counter-productive. The mistakes made in administering it were continued with steroids, its first cousin.

In today's world of sporting scandals, all the way from Michelle De Brúin to Cian O'Connor, the man in the street is perhaps more familiar with terms like steroids than he would otherwise be. Malachy is so disenchanted with such scandals, he sometimes feels that all athletes should be allowed to put whatever they want into their bodies. 'That way,' he suggests, 'at least there would be a level playing field.' The way he says it, one isn't sure if he's being tongue-in-cheek or not.

He's also perturbed about the upsurge of violence in the world. The destruction of the Twin Towers was almost Biblical in its dimension: the Towers of Babel ground to dust ... and after that the wars in Afghanistan and Iraq, bloodlust beamed into all of our homes as we digest our dinners. In today's dysfunctional world, violence has even infiltrated hospitals. The fact that an A&E unit would have a sign saying 'Patients who physically or verbally abuse medical staff will not be tolerated' would have been 'unthinkable' in his day.

He wouldn't like to be starting out again. Interns, he feels, get a raw deal. 'It takes them far too long to become specialists,' he says. But he claims he worked longer hours than they do.

Does he think the sedentary lifestyles of today's pen-pushers and computer nerds has led to more back problems than in his day? 'Not necessarily. In my experience it was the hard-working physical labourer who had the most back problems.' But of course we should all exercise as much as possible. That's common sense. (Which isn't very common, he adds.)

Is he concerned about the fact that the Irish smoke and drink too much today? 'Of course. I smoked 5 or 6 Gold Flake a day and drank a beer or two in the evenings but today's drinkers seem to drink with the sole purpose of getting drunk a lot of the time.' He stresses the fact that alcohol in moderation is beneficial to the heart and arteries. (Somehow, one doubts many Irish people are mindful of this as they enter a pub.)

He's taken good care of himself over the years and doesn't look – or act – his age. He's mentally agile and has an acute, and acerbic, sense of humour. He lives with his brother and sister-in-law in Monaghan, his study overlooking a beautiful garden. He and his brother are the only remaining Smyths left. A third brother, Kevin, who married him, passed away recently.

He's a determined man, a man who has sucked on the pap of life, who's played the hand life dealt him with resignation and matter-of-factness. Like Edith Piaf, he can say, hand on heart, 'Je ne regrette rien'. He has an elaborate lift in his house which enables him to get up and down the stairs comfortably. There are twinges in the hinges, but 'Nobody gets to my age without having something wrong with them.' The lift, one of only three in the country, is a state-of-the-art model installed by Joe O'Loughlin of Liberty Lifts. It cost a pretty penny but it's worth its weight in gold to him.

On a recent flight from New York to Dublin Dr Malachy got a thrombosis in a vein in his right leg. This was carried to his lung in the form of a clot and the lung subsequently collapsed. He was sent to Monaghan General Hospital after the plane touched down. He was diagnosed and expertly treated by a Dr B. McMahon. He got the most up-to-date treatment in the Intensive Care Unit there, better in his view than what would have been offered by a similar hospital in the U.S.

He believes nobody ever really finishes training to be a doctor. One graduates all right, but this is really only the beginning. At 90 he's still a student of sorts. He dislikes the term 'expert'. Even in the 21st century, the most esteemed specialist is, in one sense, still flying blind. He's still at the mercy of Pandora and her box of tricks.

'Because of curiosity,' he says, 'Pandora opened her box. Everything flew out as a result. Only hope stayed behind. One of the things that escaped from her box was pain, and it hasn't been recaptured yet.' In some ways he feels like Pandora himself because he produced pain and then it escaped from him. He caused it but then it scattered into a million different directions. He set the spark to a flame and caused a conflagration. The remainder of his life was devoted to trying to recruit an adequate fire brigade.

Some people, he notes, feel like lashing out at Pandora for releasing all these torments to plague us, but as he's intimated repeatedly throughout this book, he commends her for her enquiring mind. Without pain there can be no ultimate relief from pain. If it's a red light, it's also a green one.

Or, more to the point, an amber one.

Afterword

by Malachy Smyth

Sometimes I ask myself who am I at this great age of my life. Achievements have to be assessed. What have I learned, what gained? Some of my ancestors were involved in the Gold Rush outside Sacramento. They were the '49ers. Handed down to me was the conception of digging for gold, a lode that petered out. You had to assess your find, forage for nuggets. In an allegorical kind of way, I saw myself as on a long and strenuous chase. In my own way I was digging for pain. Looking back at the chase now, should I lament or rejoice? I've realised many of my goals, but too few of them to label my life an unmitigated success. I hounded pain to its lair but in the end my prey eluded me. And so the chase goes on as I hand the baton to my successors. May they continue to fight the good fight against this very tricky adversary, and one day corner him and force him to account for his (or her!) multiple onslaughts on humanity.

The main thing is to guard against smugness or arrogance, like the arrogance of the surgeon I saw in France who was afraid of time overtaking him. George Bernard Shaw once said, 'There would be very little agreement between doctors if they didn't agree to agree on the main point of the doctor always being in the right.' The point is that he isn't. Realising one's ignorance is the beginning of wisdom. There are more questions than answers. But we have to keep asking them. Maybe Pandora has another box to open for us. If so, I'll be first in the queue to examine its contents.

The nervous system controls everything in the body. It is life. Even as we sleep, the body is a hive of activity. It never goes to sleep. It never can. People don't realise how little control that they have over their own body. They don't run it. They have a say here and there but on the whole it runs despite them. The heart beats, the glands secrete, the abdominal organs work away in their myriad ways and no human hand has a voice in what is done and what isn't.

There are many types of pain. There are areas in the body where there's no pain, desert areas where very little seems to happen. There are people, as we've seen, who have virtually no sense of pain, people who experience

123

that demonic conniver playing hide-and-seek with them.

Some people in my experience believed they had tamed pain, that they could push it around and make it obey orders. It was no longer the master. This type of myopia has, ironically, a beneficial side-effect. It can help to relieve anxiety. Pain feels worse when people are anxious. The comforting thing to understand is that pain itself is a friend. It advises and it alerts us that in some part of the body something isn't working as it should.

During the war a pilot was hit by what was thought to be a piece of shrapnel but no shrapnel could be found on repeated X-rays. He did, however, have a small, almost pinhead-sized wound in the front of his wrist. It was healed when I saw him six months after the injury occurred. He was now complaining of intense pain and a burning sensation in his hand.

He could move the fingers but the hand was bluish-red in colour. It was extremely sensitive to the touch. On exploration surgically, a small piece of plastic material was found in the middle of the big nerve in front of the wrist. The fragment had penetrated into the central core of the nerve. It's here that the nerve tissue is found – a transparent tissue called the axon. It eventually passes up to the brain.

This man had in a sense a third type of pain called causalgia, which is extremely difficult to treat. The cause of his pain would appear to have been irritation from unprotected nerve tissue. I mention the incident as an illustration, yet again, that we can never take things at face value in this life. To this extent, doctors must be detectives.

Sir Arthur Conan Doyle's creation Sherlock Holmes once said, 'It is an old maxim of mine that, when you have excluded the impossible, whatever remains, however improbable, must be the truth.' In my own career I've used that procedure to some avail, narrowing my range like a dog circling a mat before he sits down. Conan Doyle also said, 'When a doctor goes wrong, he is the first of criminals'. If lawyers hang their mistakes, we bury ours. The stakes are higher in our game than any other, which is why we have to be ten times as vigilant as anyone else.

Many people feel that medicine has become too specialised today. Doctors, they say, are learning more about less and less and will one day wind up knowing practically everything about absolutely nothing. Gone are the days, they mourn, when they could get themselves 'checked out' by some Marcus Welby type of GP without copious letters of referral to higher authorities, or being placed on endless waiting lists for tests if they're not fortunate enough to be able to afford private medical insurance. There's a joke that's been going round in medical circles for some years now which concerns a doctor who refers a patient to a consultant to have his fingers counted. It isn't very funny.

Then there's the hospital trolley situation, which reached absurd proportions some time ago when a man went to the toilet only to find another patient had sabotaged his trolley when he came back. Maybe this was a wake-up call for the whole system at A&E units to be up-ended.

There's cynicism about medicine today in the same way as there's cynicism about most large structures, like the worlds of politics, religion and economics. The explosion of knowledge and access to the internet highway has also made many people feel 'Jack's as good as his master' when it comes to diagnosis. The high charges of many consultants has also resulted in charges of 'Mé Féinism' being brought against the profession. This means that when any potential scandal hits the media, like for instance the recent kerfuffle surrounding the obstetrician Michael Neary, the press has a field day with it. This isn't to suggest that such scandals shouldn't be highlighted. The recent discovery of organs being preserved for research purposes in Irish hospitals was atrocious. There have also been incidents of sexual abuse of patients, and botched operations which left many people in pain for the rest of their lives, with nobody owning up to the negligence as the wagons were circled.

Other revelations that hit the headlines were equally inexcusable, if not perhaps quite as gruesome. We may take some brief solace from the fact that they were uncovered, while being mindful of the fact that other even more damaging skeletons are laying in other cupboards as I write. There's a perception abroad that doctors, like members of other professions, will protect one another with a kind of misplaced loyalty. This has to be knocked on the head. 'You can always trust a doctor' was a comforting slogan. It may not be uttered today as frequently, or as vehemently, as heretofore, but that shouldn't stop us trying to get it back.

Conflicting reports of what's good for you and what isn't don't help the situation. One day we hear we should drink more red wine for our heart, the next we hear red wine is bad for our heart. There are horror stories about the dangers of everything from computer screens to mobile phones. One might be entitled to think that getting out of bed in the morning is injurious to one's health.

Another school of thought suggests 'Once the doctor gets his hands on you, he won't let go'. Sooner or later, if he runs enough tests, he'll find something wrong. Maybe he'll be upset if he doesn't. So your tranquil life, where everything was ticking away merrily (including your ticker) is suddenly, dramatically, transformed. From here onwards you're the 'property' of the medical establishment, to do with as they will. You're putty in their hands, and you haven't the foggiest what sinister things they're finding inside your body. (Or, if you're of a paranoid persuasion, actually putting there.)

Some people claim that after they bring their car to a garage for a service, it performs worse afterwards instead of better. The implication is that the mechanic did something underhand to increase his profits. Could it be conceivable that a doctor would descend to such devious depths? Films like *The Hospital* and *Coma* play around with such notions, which doesn't do much to enhance the status of medicine. When I was young – don't ask me how long ago that is – we had a joke about a man who took over his father's medical practice. After his first day in the surgery he said beamingly to his father, 'I've cured Mrs Gilhooley.' Mrs Gilhooley being a rich dowager who had been keeping Daddy's pockets lined for many years with one spurious complaint after another, this wasn't exactly music to his ears. 'You blithering idiot,' the senior practitioner barked at his son, 'I left her to you as a legacy.' Boom boom.

'The three most important things in medicine,' a noted surgeon once said, 'are diagnosis, diagnosis and diagnosis. The treatment can be looked up in a book.' This is fine if we're dealing with a patient etherised upon a table, but when he or she wakes up, different strategies of behaviour may be called for. Indeed, knowing the personality of the patient might well help in the diagnosis, particularly if there's a psychosomatic element present. As the Oxford surgeon William Osler once put it, 'Knowing the patient that has the disease is just as important as knowing the disease the patient has.' Maybe that's what's disappearing from medicine today as it becomes more depersonalised. I saw signs of it decades ago when the 'red carpet treatment' was given to operating theatre posers who paraded before me almost without their feet touching the ground, legends in their own lunchtimes. They were as addicted to power, I would wager, almost as much as the serial killer Harold Shipman. Their fantasy was to play God. Many of them succeeded in convincing themselves they had realised that fantasy.

Such men seemed to be more interested in bold flourishes than the well-being of the patients under their care. Thankfully they were in the minority but today's logistics may strengthen their numbers. Few doctors today seem to have the time to talk about 'the weather' with their patients. In rural areas I know of many people who frequent their local G.P. for precisely this reason. It would be indeed cruel to dub them time-wasters but sometimes this is their plight. If they're medical card holders, the thinking goes, the danger is all the greater that they'll get short shrift from an ambitious intern who's already thinking about his pay cheque, or the next person waiting outside the door to benefit from his 'expertise'.

People also understandably feel that there's too much bluntness in medicine today when it comes to the imparting of information. I heard of one man who was informed his wife was terminally ill on a public corridor within the earshot of a number of other people who had nothing to do with her. This is deplorable behaviour masquerading as 'transparency' – a perverse attempt to act as a corollary to the coyness of yesteryear concerning such delicate matters. Transparency is fine until it becomes callousness. It's a delicate line to tread.

John Dorgan once said the definition of an orthopaedic surgeon was somebody with 'the strength of an ox, but half the brain'. He was joking - I hope - but no more than Shaw, his comment should act as a salutary reminder to us about our fallibility. Maybe an age that's seen Harold Shipman is continually reminded of this anyway, though maybe the fear of litigation has swung the tide too far the other way – i.e. the doctor is guilty until proven innocent. If we have to accept this, so be it. The point is that we're all just scratching the surface. We need patients to help us just as they need us to help them. The good thing about medicine today is that it's more interactive than when I was practising. There may be less reverence for the doctor but there's also less fear, and that has to be a plus. People want more answers today; they'll take the doctor on. (Doctor to patient: 'The cheque you gave me last week came back.' Patient: 'So did the pain!')

People live longer today, that's a fact. Sixty, as they say, is the new fifty. But other ailments that we didn't have before plague us. They still haven't found a vaccine for AIDS after twenty years. It's like the new TB. Stress is another killer. People always had stress, of course, but it seems to have gone into another league today. Are people less able to handle their problems today than in yesteryear? Perhaps. There seems to be less determination, less ability to soak up discomfort. We've cushioned ourselves with so many creature comforts, we've lost some inner resolve.

In any case, I hope you enjoy reading about my life as much as I've enjoyed living it. Maybe you think I'm just an old grouch but I still have strong feelings about what we're doing to our bodies. Suffering is inevitable, needless to say, but a lot of it is preventable too. It upsets me deeply to see athletes, for instance, looking for a quick fix for their problems instead of a more long-term solution. This again is the modern disease: we want everything yesterday. But a little foresight can prolong any sportsman's career. Likewise for those suffering from back problems. In my day rest was prescribed, today exercise is preferred. Somebody once said our back problems began the day we came down from the trees. Perhaps we should ask the monkeys their view on this. They might agree that *homo erectus* was a bad idea. But how do you go back with your back? (That't a bad pun.)

'Be careful what health books you read,' Mark Twain warned us, 'You may die of a misprint.' Indeed. And maybe that applies to this one too. It was certainly relevant to me at the convention I attended where I was mistaken for the deceased M.J. Smyth. Thankfully that was resolved and I reclaimed my small perch on the totem pole of research. If we're all fumbling in the darkness, I hope I've fumbled as well as my colleagues. That's the only type of recognition I want to lay claim to. Each time we fail, Samuel Beckett advised us, we should try to fail better. It's a humble ambition but a realistic one. Great achievements begin slowly. A small step for man, a giant leap for mankind.

Albert Schweitzer once said, 'We must all die, but if I can save man from days of torture, that is my great and ever-new privilege.' He went on to call pain 'a more terrible lord of mankind than even death himself.' Such words have sustained me as I've made my way through my adventurous life, carried along like a leaf in a storm through its various vicissitudes.

* * *